Step by Step into a Deeper Walk in Christ

By: Sandra Lott

An Interactive Devotional

May God always
bless you +
Keep you!

Sandra Lott

Step by Step into a Deeper Walk In Christ: An Interactive Devotional by Sandra Lott

Published by Pen It! Publications, LLC
812-371-4128 www.penitpublications.com

Published in the United States of America by Pen It! Publications, LLC

ISBN: 978-1-949609-37-0

Cover by Donna Cook

"And you shall seek Me, and find Me, when you shall search for Me with all your heart."
(Jeremiah 29:13)

Follow Me

Come and follow Me no matter who
you are or what you have done.
Just take up your cross and follow Me.

Come and follow Me through life's many
trials, and if you love Me faithfully,
by your side is where I'll always be!

Come and follow Me down roads of many
paths, if you stay with Me and always true,
I will always be right here waiting for you.

Just come and follow Me!

Table of Contents

Introduction 6

Connect to Each Other... 13

Chapter 1: Soaking 17

Chapter 2: "I Am" 45

Chapter 3: The Cross: Salvation................................ 147

Chapter 4: Prayer Life.. 161

Chapter 5: Admit-I Did What? Sin & Forgiveness 171

Chapter 6: Surrender! Oh No!................................... 183

Chapter 7: Rocky Road Ahead: Trials 195

Chapter 8: Conquered Trails: Growth 207

Chapter 9: Stepping Out... 217

Chapter 10: Dunked!.. 229

Chapter 11: Deeper Still 241

Chapter 12: Give Thanks 257

Final Thoughts 269

Other Books By Sandra Lott....................................... 274

God Loves You!... 275

Invitation to Salvation Prayer.................................... 278

Introduction

*I*f you are reading this book, then you have made the decision to draw closer to the Lord. I applaud your decision, it will be the best thing you have ever done. Walking in His presence every day, being sensitive to His Spirit, will help you in your everyday life. "Submit yourselves, then, to God. Resist the devil, and he will flee from you. Come near to God, and he will come near to you. Wash your hands, you sinners, and purify your hearts, you double-minded. Grieve, mourn, and wail. Change your laughter to mourning, and your joy to gloom. Humble yourselves before the Lord, and he will lift you up." (James 4:7-10)

This is a different kind of devotional. This one is interactive, meaning you will take part of it, and it is one that is meant to savor, so to take your time. There is no time limit, take as long as you want with each chapter. Dive into each chapter, and let what the Lord is trying to teach you through them soak into your spirit. Take the question that is presented, and pray and ask the Lord, "What are you trying to teach me, say or reveal to me in this question?" Then wait patiently in His presence, and allow Him time to speak to your heart. "But if we hope for what we do not yet have, we wait for it patiently." (Romans 8:25) The more time you spend with the Lord the more you will get to know Him and His love for you. Knowing that is victory, because no matter how hard life gets, when you know beyond the shadow of any doubt that He loves you, then you will be able to withstand anything the devil throws at you and come out victoriously!

In any relationship you did not know that person completely at your first meeting. You took time to get to know each other whether it was someone that would turn out to be your best friend, or your spouse. You put time and effort into getting to know them. You spent time with each other, you talked and asked questions, and you also listened. Communication is two ways.

God wants to talk to you! Do you take the time just to listen? "Jesus answered, "It is written: 'Man shall not live on bread alone, but on every word that comes from the mouth of God." (Matthew 4:4) He will speak to your heart and when He does, you will know it. "My sheep hear My voice, and I know them, and they follow Me." (John 10:27) There will be a peace and a gentle warmth, you will know it is Him, and every word will line up with His Word. "They asked each other, "Were not our hearts burning within us while he talked with us on the road and opened the Scriptures to us?" (Luke 24:32)Take the time as you read through this book to truly get to know God, to talk and pray and listen. You will find Him when you seek Him with all of your heart.

"For I know the plans I have for you," declares the Lord, "plans to prosper you and not to harm you, plans to give you hope and a future. Then you will call on me, and come and pray to me, and I will listen to you. You will seek me and find me when you seek me with all your heart. I will be found by you," declares the Lord, "and will bring you back from captivity. I will gather you from all the nations and places where I have banished you," declares the Lord, "and will bring you back to the place from which I carried you into exile." (Jeremiah 29:11-14)

The slower you take this, taking time to dive in and allow the Holy Spirit to take this journey with you, talking and listening, the more you will get out it! You don't need the answers to all your questions at once. Take time to get in His presence and you will be blessed!

Sandra Lott

Shadow of Your Wings

Take me away from this world and into your presence,
it is where I feel at home, it is where I belong.
It is where I've belonged all along.

Hide me in the shadow of your wings
guide me in the light of your path,
it is there that your joy and peace reside in me
and keeps me forever free!

Take me away Lord and hide me in your wings.
Shine your love into my heart and
your praises I will sing.

Take me away O Lord I pray.
Hide me in the shadow of your
presence every day!

I Don't Need All The Answers In A Day

I don't have to find all the answers in a day.
You will walk with me side by side and
Hand in hand and guide me on my way.
You will light up my path with each step that I take.
I don't have to find all the answers in a day.

Little by little with each step I take
You light up my path and give me clear
Vision and guide me on my way.
The answers begin to come, and the path is revealed.
My faith keeps growing as I walk in the light of Your path
Confidently taking each step;
I trust You to light up my way.

I know I don't have to find all the answers in a day.

Step by Step

Step by Step You lead me. Step by step I follow.
You lead me in the everlasting way.

Though darkness may surround; the light of Your
glory illuminates my path.

Darkness is not dark to You,
in childlike faith I follow.

Though darkness may surround; darkness is not dark to You.
The light of Your glory lights my way.

So, step by step I follow.
You lead me in the way everlasting.

Step by Step You lead me. Step by step I follow.
You lead me in the everlasting way.
You bore my sins, you wore my pain; in it I am healed.

By the cross You carried all my sins, all my pain &
all my worries are nailed to it. So, step by step I follow.

You rose to glory and left life, liberty, and purity behind
Through Your Holy Spirit; so, step by step I follow.

Step by Step You lead me. Step by step I follow.
You lead me in the everlasting way until finally those
Steps lead me home.

Step By Step Into A Deeper Walk in Christ

Connect to Each Other

$\mathcal{I}$ hope you will be inspired as you journey through this book into a deep walk with the Lord. But, guess what? It does not have to end with each chapter. Below are different ways you can connect online through a Facebook page or my Webpage devoted to this book. You can connect in the ways suggested or one of your own. Be inspired by the revelations of other readers.

Here is the link to the Facebook page:

https://www.facebook.com/stepbystepintoadeeperwalkinChrist

As you post a comment to the webpage I will post it into the page itself. You can share your revelations as well as receive encouragement for that of others.

Here is the link to the webpage:

https://sandralott.wordpress.com/stepbystep

CHAPTER 1: Soaking

Connect: Post a verse from this chapter each day on the FB page along with how the verse spoke to your heart.

CHAPTER 2: "I AM"

Connect: Post one of the names of God on the FB page each day as you read and comment on how God has been that to you.

CHAPTER 3: The Cross: Salvation

Connect: Post to the FB page what the cross means to and share your testimony!

CHAPTER 4: Prayer Life

Connect: Post to the FB a heartfelt prayer to God, or ways this devotion has helped you to add meaning to your prayer life.

CHAPTER 5: Admit: I Did What? Sin & Forgiveness

Connect: Post to the FB how this devotion helped you to search yourself and also make amends.

CHAPTER 6: Surrender! Oh No!

Connect: Post to the FB the issues you have had in the past surrendering. How has this devotion inspired you to seek God's help in surrendering?

CHAPTER 7: Rocky Road Ahead: Trials

Connect: Post to the FB any new revelations you have learned through this devotion about going through trials and how to stay hopeful during them.

CHAPTER 8: Conquered Trails: Growth

Connect: Post to the FB some of the many things you have learned through the trials you have been through.

CHAPTER 9: Stepping Out

Connect: Post to the FB page the inspirations God has spoken to your heart as you read through this devotion. Has He given you any new ways you can step out and be His heart?

CHAPTER 10: Dunked!

Connect: Post to the FB if you have been baptized in the Holy Spirit and the difference it has made in your Christian walk. If you have not, post any new revelations the Holy Spirit revealed to you about being baptized.

CHAPTER 11: Deeper Still

Connect: Post to the FB some of the many things you have learned through about taking time to listen to God.

CHAPTER 12: Give Thanks

Connect: Post to the FB as a message to God and your thanks to Him in your daily life.

Chapter 1
Soaking

*I*t is a beautiful sunny day outside, and you decide to go
to the nearest park to soak in the rays of the sun. It is not
too hot, and there is a cool, gentle breeze. You find a big
tree with branches that hang over like an umbrella.
"Perfect!" You shout, and proceed to lay out your blanket,
and pull out your book for some well needed alone time to
soak up the rays of the sun.

That is what this chapter is all about, soaking in the rays,
the love, of the Son. Do you remember the time when you
first met that special someone, or your best friend? Do
you remember how you could spend hours, all day even,
talking to them? You wanted to find out all you could.
That is what this chapter will do for you. You are soaking
in the love of God. Take a whole month for this, or as
long as you want. There is no time table; this is quality
time between you and God. The more time you take to
soak in His love for you the more you get to know Him,
which will help you walk through every situation in life that
comes your way victoriously.

Part of deepening your relationship with Him is knowing who He is and just how much He loves you. That confidence will help you to have an unshakeable spirit and spiritual walk. "If you continue in the faith grounded and settled, and be not moved away from the hope of the gospel, which you have heard, and which was preached to every creature who is under heaven; of which I Paul am made a minister." (Colossians 1:23)

On the next few pages you will find scriptures on God's love for you, for mankind. Take the time to read through the verses every day, but do not rush, this is not a race. This is an exercise to deepen your intimacy and walk in Christ, so to fully experience it, you need to truly soak in each verse as if you were soaking in the rays of the sun on a beautiful day in the park. As you read each verse, insert your name where applicable and read it out loud. This will help it to soak into your heart as well. "So, then faith comes by hearing, and hearing by the word of God." (Romans 10:17)

There are also lines after each verse for you to take notes, make a comment or a word that the Holy Spirit may want to speak to you regarding that verse. Pray and ask the Holy Spirit to speak to you regarding this verse then listen and allow Him to speak to your heart. "Ask and you will receive, and your joy will be complete." (John 16:24) Personalize it and allow His love to penetrate thoroughly.

Scriptures on God's Love

1. Exodus 15: 13-14 -- "In Your unfailing love You will lead the people You have redeemed. In Your strength You will guide them to Your holy dwelling. The nations will hear and tremble."

_____

_____

_____

2. Exodus 34: 6-7 -- "The Lord, the Lord, the compassionate and gracious God, slow to anger, abounding in love and faithfulness, maintaining love to thousands, and forgiving wickedness, rebellion and sin."

_____

_____

_____

3. Numbers 14:18 -- "The Lord is slow to anger, abounding in love and forgiving sin and rebellion."

_____

_____

_____

4. Deuteronomy 5:10 -- "but showing love to a thousand generations, of those who love Me and keep My commandments."

_____

_____

_____

5. Deuteronomy 7:7 -- "The Lord did not set His affections on you and chose you because you were more numerous than other peoples, for you were the fewest of all peoples. But it was because the Lord loved you and kept the oath He swore to your forefathers that He brought you out with a mighty hand and redeemed you from the land of slavery, from the power of Pharaoh King of Egypt."

_____

_____

_____

6. Deuteronomy 7:9 -- "Know therefore that the Lord your God is God, He is the faithful God, keeping His covenant of love to a thousand generations of those who love Him and keep His commands."

_____

_____

_____

7. Deuteronomy 7:12-13-- "If you pay attention to these laws and are careful to follow them, then the Lord your God will keep His covenant of love with you as He swore to your forefathers. He will love you and bless you and increase your numbers."

_____

_____

_____

8. Deuteronomy 10:15 -- "Yet the Lord set His affection on your forefathers and loved them, and He chose you, their descendants, above all the nations, as it is today."

_____

_____

_____

9. Deuteronomy 10:18 -- "He defends the cause of the fatherless and the widow, and loves the alien, giving him food and clothing"

_____

_____

_____

10. Deuteronomy 23:5 -- "However, the Lord your God would not listen to Balaam but turned the curse into a blessing for you, because the Lord your God loves you."

_____

_____

_____

11. I Chronicles 16:34 -- "Give thanks to the Lord, for He is good; His love endures forever."

_____

_____

_____

12. Psalm 25:6 -- "Remember, O Lord, you great mercy and love, for they are from old."

_____

_____

_____

13. Psalm 25:10 -- "All the ways of the Lord are loving and faithful for those who keep the demands of His covenant."

_____

_____

_____

14. Psalm 36:5 -- "Your love, O Lord, reaches to the heavens, your faithfulness to the skies."

_____

_____

_____

15. Psalm 37:28 -- "For the Lord loves the just and will not forsake His faithful ones. They will be protected forever."

_____

_____

_____

16. Psalm 44:3 -- "It was not by their sword that they won the land, nor did their arm bring them victory; it was your right hand, your arm, and the light of your face, for you loved them."

_____

_____

_____

17. Psalm 57:10 -- "For great is your love, reaching to the heavens; your faithfulness reaches to the skies."

_____

_____

_____

18. Psalm 66:20 -- "Praise be to God, who has not rejected my prayer or withheld His love from me!"

_____

_____

_____

19. Psalm 103:11 -- "For as high as the heavens are above the earth, so great is His love for those who fear Him."

_____

_____

_____

20. Psalm 108:6 "Save us and help us with your right hand that those you love may be delivered."

_____

_____

_____

21. Psalm 117:1-2 "Praise the Lord, all you nations; extol Him, all you peoples. For great is His love toward us, and the faithfulness of the Lord endures forever. Praise the Lord."

_____

_____

_____

22.   Psalm 136 "Give thanks to the Lord, for he is good. His love endures forever. Give thanks to the God of gods. His love endures forever. Give thanks to the Lord of lords: His love endures forever. to him who alone does great wonders, His love endures forever. who by his understanding made the heavens, His love endures forever. who spread out the earth upon the waters, His love endures forever. Who made the great lights—His love endures forever. the sun to govern the day, His love endures forever. the moon and stars to govern the night; His love endures forever. To him who struck down the firstborn of Egypt His love endures forever. And brought Israel out from among them His love endures forever. With a mighty hand and outstretched arm; His love endures forever. To him who divided the Red Sea asunder His love endures forever. And brought Israel through the midst of it, His love endures forever. But swept Pharaoh and his army into the Red Sea; His love endures forever. To him who led his people through the wilderness; His love endures forever. To him who struck down great kings, His love endures forever. And killed mighty kings—His love endures forever. Sihon king of the Amorites His love endures forever. And Og king of Bashan—His love endures forever. And gave their land as an inheritance, His love endures forever. An inheritance to his servant Israel. His love endures forever. He remembered us in our low estate His love endures forever. And freed us from our enemies. His love endures forever. He gives food to every creature. His love endures forever. Give thanks to the God of heaven. His love endures forever."

_____

_____

_____

23. Psalm 138:1-3 -- "I will praise You, O Lord, with all my heart; before the "gods" I will sing Your praise. I will bow down toward Your holy temple and will praise Your name for Your love and Your faithfulness, for You have exalted above all things Your name and Your Word. When I called, You answered me; You made me bold and stouthearted."

_____

_____

_____

24. Psalm 138:6-8 -- "Though the Lord is on high, He looks upon the lowly, but the proud He knows from afar. Though I walk in the midst of trouble, You preserve my life; You stretch out Your hand against the anger of my foes, with Your right hand You save me. The Lord will fulfill His purpose for me; Your love, O Lord, endures forever- do not abandon the works of Your hands."

_____

_____

_____

25. Psalm 145:13 -- "The Lord is faithful to all His promises and loving toward all He has made."

_____

_____

_____

26. Proverbs 3:11-12 -- "My son, do not despise the Lord's discipline and do not resent His rebuke, because the Lord disciplines those He loves, as a father the son he delights in."

_____

_____

_____

27.   Proverbs 8: 17 -- "I love those who love Me, and those who seek Me find Me."

_____

_____

_____

28. Proverbs 16:6 -- "Through love and faithfulness sin is atoned for; through the fear of the Lord a man avoids evil."

_____

_____

_____

29. Isaiah 54:10 -- "Though the mountains be shaken, and the hills be removed, yet My unfailing love for you will not be shaken nor My covenant of peace be removed," says the Lord, who has compassion on you."

_____

_____

_____

30. Jeremiah 31:3 -- "I have loved you with and everlasting love; I have drawn you with loving kindness."

_____

_____

_____

31.   Lamentations 3:22 -- "Because of the Lord's great love we are not consumed, for His compassion never fails."

_____

_____

_____

32.   Lamentations 3: 32-33 -- "Though He brings grief, He will show compassion, so great is His unfailing love for He does not willingly bring affliction or grief to the children of men."

_____

_____

_____

33. Zephaniah 3:17 -- "The Lord your God is with you, He is mighty to save. He will take great delight in you, He will quiet you with His love, He will rejoice over you with singing."

_____

_____

_____

34. John 3:16 -- "For God so loved the world that He gave His One and Only Son, that whoever believes in Him shall not perish but have eternal life."

_____

_____

_____

35. John 5:20-21 -- "For the Father loves the Son and shows Him all He does. Yes, to your amazement He will show Him even greater things than these. For just as the Father raises the dead and gives them life, even so the Son gives life to whom He is pleased to give it."

_____

_____

_____

36. John 14:21 -- "Whoever has My commands and obeys them, He is the one who loves Me. He who loves Me will be loved by My Father, and I too will love him and show Myself to him."

_____

_____

_____

37. John 15:12-13 -- "Love each other as I have loved you. Greater love has no one than this that he lay down his life for his friends."

_____

_____

_____

38. **Romans 5: 2-5** -- "And we rejoice in the hope of the glory of God not only so, but we also rejoice in our sufferings, because we know that suffering produces perseverance; perseverance, character; and character, hope. And hope does not disappoint us, because God has poured out His love into our hearts by the Holy Spirit, whom He has given us."

_____

_____

_____

39. **Romans 5:8** -- "But God demonstrates His own love for us in this: while we were still sinners, Christ died for us."

_____

_____

_____

40. **Romans 8:37-39** -- "No, in all these things we are more than conquerors through Him who loved us. For I am convinced that neither death nor life, neither angels nor demons, neither the present nor the future, nor any powers, neither height nor depth, nor anything else in all creation, will be able to separate us from the love of God that is in Christ Jesus our Lord."

_____

_____

_____

41. I Corinthians 2:9 -- "No eye has seen, no ear has heard, no mind has conceived what God has prepared for those who love Him."

_____

_____

_____

42. Galatians 2:20 -- "The life I live in the body, I live by faith in the Son of God, who loved me and gave Himself for me."

_____

_____

_____

43.   Ephesians 1:4-6 -- "For He chose us in Him before the creation of the world to be holy and blameless in His sight. In love He predestined us to be adopted as His sons through Jesus Christ, in accordance with His pleasure and will-- to the praise of His glorious grace, which He has freely given us in the One He loves."

_____

_____

_____

44.   Ephesians 2:4 -- "But because of His great love for us, God, who is rich in mercy, made us alive with Christ even when we were dead in transgressions-- it is by grace you have been saved."

_____

_____

_____

45.   Ephesians 3:17-19 -- "And I pray that you, being rooted and established in love, may have power together with all the saints, to grasp how wide and long and high and deep is the love of Christ, and to know this love that surpasses knowledge-- that you be filled to the measure of all the fullness of God."

_____

_____

_____

46. Ephesians 5:1-2 -- "Be imitators of God, therefore, as dearly loved children and live a life of love, just as Christ loved us and gave Himself up for us as a fragrant offering and sacrifice to God."

_____

_____

_____

47. II Thessalonians 2:13 -- "But we ought always to thank God for you, brothers loved by the Lord, because from the beginning God chose you to be saved through the sanctifying work of the Spirit and through belief in the truth."

_____

_____

_____

48. II Thessalonians 2:16 -- "May our Lord Jesus Christ Himself and God our Father, who loved us and by His grace gave us eternal encouragement and good hope, encourage your hearts and strengthen you in every good deed and word."

_____

_____

_____

49. Hebrews 12: 5-6 -- "My son, do not make light of the Lord's discipline, and do not lose heart when He rebukes you, because the Lord disciplines those He loves, and He punishes everyone He accepts as a son."

_____

_____

_____

50. James 1: 12 -- "Blessed is the man who perseveres under trial, because when he has stood the test, he will receive the crown of life that God has promised to those who love Him."

_____

_____

_____

51. I John 3: 1-- "How great is the love the Father has lavished on us that we should be called children of God!"

_____

_____

_____

52. I John 4: 7-10 -- "Dear friends, let us love one another, for love comes from God. Everyone who loves has been born of God and knows God. Whoever does not love does not know God, because God is love. This is how God showed His love among us: He sent His One and Only Son into the world that we might live through Him. This is love: not that we loved God, but that He loved us and sent His Son as an atoning sacrifice for our sins."

_____

_____

_____

53. I John 4: 19 -- "We love because He first loved us."

_____

_____

_____

54. I John 4:15-17 -- "If anyone acknowledges that Jesus is the Son of God, God lives in Him and He in God. And so we know and rely on the love God has for us. God is love. Whoever lives in love lives in God, and God in Him. In this way, love is made complete among us so that we will have confidence on the Day of Judgment, because in the world we are like Him."

_____

_____

---

55. II John 1-3 -- "To the chosen lady and her children, whom I love in the truth-- and not I only, but also all who know the truth, which lives in us and will be with us forever: Grace, mercy and peace from God the Father and from Jesus Christ, the Father's Son, will be with us in truth and love."

---

56. Jude 1-2 -- "To those who have been called, who are loved by God the Father and kept by Jesus Christ: mercy, peace and love be yours in abundance."

---

57. Revelation 3:19 -- "Those whom I love I rebuke and discipline. So be earnest and repent."

_____

_____

_____

As you read through these verses, did you learn anything new, about what you may have believed before? Has the Lord revealed anything to you about how much He loves you? Maybe a past trauma broke your heart, and subconsciously you transferred that pain, and inability to trust anyone onto God. Has He revealed the truth in His unconditional love to you? God is love and He cannot go against His true nature. Let that piece of knowledge seep into your heart. Record any new thoughts and comments on the lines below. This will help you to remember and also to remind yourself later when the enemy tries to fill you with lies.

_____

_____

_____

_____

Sandra Lott

Facebook Connect: Post a verse from this chapter each day on the FB page along with how the verse spoke to your heart.

Chapter 2
"I Am"

God told Moses to call Him, "I Am," in Exodus 3:14 when Moses asked Him who to say sent him. That is because whatever we need that is what He is to us. Knowing who He is to YOU, will also help you to draw closer to Him, as well as knowing how you can rely on Him and what for. So, in this chapter we are going to go through some of the many names of God and what they represent. Each different name for God will have a short devotion. As you read through them ask the Holy Spirit to remind you of past situations that He showed up as one of the many names below, which represents the many facets of who He is to us, and allow Him to speak to your spirit. Record your thoughts and remembrances on the lines following.

1. Jehovah: Self-Existing One: Lord

(Exodus 3:14) "God said to Moses, 'I Am Who I Am. This is what you are to say to the Israelites" 'I Am has sent me to you."

God is our Creator and the reason why we even exist. From ancient of days, He was, He is, and always will be; Self Existent One. He is our Savior, and there is no other name but the name of Jesus His son by which men are saved. "Salvation is found in no one else, for there is no other name under heaven given to men by which we must be saved." (Acts 4:12) Our God is whatever we need Him to be which is why He told Moses to tell the Israelites "I Am has sent me to you." He is our God and our Lord most importantly. When we have God on our side we will always have victory. "Then Asa called to the Lord his God and said, 'Lord, there is no one like You to help the powerless against the mighty. Help us, O Lord our God, for we rely on You, and in Your name, we have come against this vast army. O Lord, You are our God; do not let man prevail against You." (II Chronicles 14:11)

Our God is the same and does not change; His love is constant and forever; He does not change; we do. "For I, the Lord, do not change; therefore you, O sons of Jacob, are not consumed." (Malachi 3:6)

"Jesus Christ is the same yesterday and today and forever." (Hebrews 13:8) If Jesus is the same yesterday, today and forever, so is His Holy Spirit and the anointing He places on everyone born into the family of God. He is our Guide, He satisfies our needs and gives us strength. "The Lord will guide you always; He will satisfy your needs in a sun-scorched land and will strengthen your frame." (Isaiah 58:11) This means even when you are going through a really rough trial and you are feeling weak and overwhelmed, trust God to strengthen you and be with you through it all. "The Lord is with me; I will not be afraid. What can man do to me?" (Psalm 118:6)

He is our Rock and is from everlasting to everlasting. "Trust in Jehovah forever, for in God the I Am, we have an everlasting Rock." (Isaiah 26:4) This means His love is eternal, never changing and never will He stop loving us, "Who shall separate us from the love of Christ? Shall trouble or hardship or persecution or famine or nakedness or danger or sword? As it is written: 'For your sake we face death all day long; we are considered a sheep to be slaughtered.' No, in all these things we are more than conquerors through Him who loved us. For I am convinced that neither death nor life, neither angels nor demons, neither the present nor the future, nor any powers, neither height nor depth, nor anything else in all creation will be able to separate us from the love of God that is in Christ Jesus our Lord." (Romans 8:35-39)

God is love and He is everything we need, from creation, to salvation, our physical needs, spiritual needs, deliverance, guidance, comfort, wisdom, understanding and grace. Think about it, was there a time, when He came through for you? You felt helpless and hopeless, you were not even sure how to pray, you just knew you needed help and cried out, "Jesus, help me!" Ask Him to remind you of those times and record it so you look back on it and be encouraged.

_____

_____

_____

_____

_____

_____

_____

_____

_____

_____

_____

_____

_____

2. Adonai: The Lord

(Genesis 15:1-2) "After this, the Word of the Lord came to Abram in a vision: 'Do not be afraid, Abram. I am your shield, your very great reward.' But Abram said, 'O Sovereign Lord, what can you give me since I remain childless and the one who will inherit my estate is Eliezer of Damascus?'"

Jesus Christ, is He the Lord of your life? You say, "Yes I asked Him into my heart," but do you live it? Is He the Lord of your mouth? "But now you must rid yourselves of all such things as these: anger, rage, malice, slander and filthy language from your lips." (Colossians 3:8) Do you gossip in the name of concern? "A perverse man stirs up dissension, and a gossip separates close friends." (Proverbs 16:28) Does your language get the best of you when you get mad? Is He truly the Lord of your life? Is He the Lord of your thoughts? Do you take captive every thought to the obedience of Jesus Christ? "We demolish arguments and every pretension that sets itself up against the knowledge of God, and we take captive every thought to make it obedient to Christ." (II Corinthians 10:5) Are the thoughts you let permeate your mind worse than your mouth ever was, or maybe even worse than it is now? Is Jesus truly the Lord of your life? Is He, Adonai, your Lord, your Master and Savior and the one you truly love and adore and long to please? "These people come near to Me with their mouth and honor Me with their lips, but their hearts are far from Me. Their worship of Me is made up only of rules taught by men." (Isaiah 29:13) Whatever has your devotion, whatever controls you, whatever you just cannot live without is your lord or your master. "For a man is a slave to whatever has mastered him." Is Jesus your Master? What about your body, do you go to church on Sunday then out of preserving a relationship and not wanting to make waves you take part in smoking and drinking and then you tell yourself, "I don't really like it and it is only once in a while?" (II Peter 2:19)

Is He truly your Master, Adonai? What about your time? When an opportunity presents itself to be of some help to someone, does your comfort come first? Do you reach out and be the hands and feet of Christ? Where would we all be if He just stayed home instead out of obedience and love, He came to earth to die for us? "Greater love has no one than this, that he lay down his life for his friends." (John 15:13) Where would we be? "For God so loved the world that He gave His One and Only Son, that whoever believes in Him shall not perish but have eternal life. For God did not send His Son into the world to condemn the world, but to save the world through Him." (John 3:16-17)

Is He truly Adonai to you? Do you get up extra early when something fun comes along or your boss needs you, but are always tired or just too busy to spend time with

God in the Word, or just in conversation? He is your Lord when you need something but when things are going great, His Word has no place in your life? Don't you know that just as food is nourishment to your body, the Word is nourishment to your soul? It is your "bread of life." "I am the bread of life. He who comes to Me will never go hungry, and he who believes in Me will never be thirsty." (John 6:35) Is He truly your Lord, Adonai? Is He Lord over all in your heart, soul, mind, body and life? "But God demonstrates His own love for us in this: While we were still sinners, Christ died for us." (Romans 5:8) God's love for mankind is the greatest and most unselfish love you will ever experience or receive. He loved us first; do you appreciate His love? Is your heart and mind overwhelmed with love and devotion for Him no matter what you are going through?

Is He your Adonai? Is He your Lord? Have you come to a place where pleasing Him is much more important than what others think of you? Is He more important than the consequences you may suffer if you "do not go along?" Ask the Holy Spirit to reveal to you areas you may need to work on. Record them and then pray, repent if needed, and ask for His help.

_____

_____

_____

_____

_____

_____

_____

_____

_____

_____

_____

_____

_____

_____

3. El Shaddai: God Almighty

(Genesis 17:1) "When Abram was ninety-nine years old, the Lord appeared to him and said, 'I am El-Shaddai— 'God Almighty.' Serve Me faithfully, and live a blameless life."

The most wonderful part of being a Christian is being a child of God. Do you ever think about that? God

Almighty, Creator of everything is also your Heavenly Father; God Almighty, All-powerful, All-knowing and Ever-present! There is nowhere that you can go, that God will not be there to watch over you and protect you. "Where can I go from Your Spirit? Where can I go from Your presence? If I go up to the heavens, you are there; if I make my bed in the depths, You are there. If I rise on the wings of the dawn, if I settle on the far side of the sea, even there Your hand will guide me, Your right hand will hold me fast." (Psalm 139:7-10) God is everything to me; He is my Friend, I tell Him everything. He is my Father who supplies all my needs, "Taste and see that the Lord is good; blessed is the man who takes refuge in Him. Fear the Lord, you His saints, for those who fear Him lack nothing. The lions may grow weak and hungry, but those who seek the Lord lack no good thing." (Psalm 34:8-10)

He is my God and I worship Him, "But I, by Your great mercy, will come into Your house; in reverence will I bow down toward Your holy temple." (Psalm 5:7) He is my deliverer who saves and protects me from trouble, "A righteous man may have many troubles, but the Lord delivers him from them all; He protects all his bones, not one of them will be broken." (Psalm 34:19-20) He is my Savior; through Jesus Christ His only Son, my sins are atoned for, "For God so loved the world that He gave His One and Only Son, that whoever believes in Him shall not perish but have eternal life." (John 3:16) El Shaddai means God Almighty, "Holy, holy, holy is the Lord God Almighty, who was, and is, and is to come." (Revelations 4:8)

Are you surrounded by trouble? Are you overwhelmed in your finances, emotions from past heartaches, relationship trouble or trouble with your children? Then come to the Lord God Almighty! Give yourself completely to Him and let Him care for you, guide you, correct you and create a new spirit within you. Come to the Almighty and let Him give you rest, "He who dwells in the shelter of the Most High will rest in the shadow of the Almighty." (Psalm 91:1)

What areas of your life do you need God Almighty to show up in? Have there been times in the past that He showed up in such a great way, it truly brought Him glory and awe to your heart? Write those times down or if you need to now, write your prayer to Him below.

_____

_____

_____

_____

_____

_____

_____

_____

_____

_____

_____

_____

_____

_____

4. El Elyon: Most High God

(Psalm 78:35) "They remembered that God was their Rock, that God Most High was their Redeemer."

Our Almighty God in heaven is the only One true God and there is no other. (Isaiah 45:5) "I am the Lord, and there is no other; apart from Me there is no God." Only the One true God is the creator of all mankind. (Isaiah 44:24) "This is what the Lord says—I am the Lord, who has made all things, who alone stretched out the heavens, who spread out the earth by Myself." He is the only One true God is the One the Most High God who is All-Knowing and Omniscient. (I John 3:20) "For God is greater than our hearts and He knows everything."

He is the Alpha and Omega (Revelation 22:13) "I am the Alpha and Omega, the First and the Last, the Beginning and the End." He knows the end from the beginning (Isaiah 46:10) "I make known the end from the beginning, from ancient times, what is still to come. I say: My purpose will stand, and I will do all that I please." He is Spirit, and is Ever-present. He is the One and Only Most High God; Creator of all things and all things answer to His command. (Mark 4:41) "Who is this? Even the wind and the waves obey Him?" There is no other God besides our God, the only living God who by Himself saw that there was no one to redeem mankind so, He did it Himself. (Isaiah 59:16-17) "He saw that there was no one, He was appalled that there was no one to intervene; so, His own arm worked salvation for Him, and His own righteousness sustained Him. He put on the righteousness as His breastplate, and the helmet of salvation on His head; He put on the garments of vengeance and wrapped Himself in zeal as in a cloak."

This is the greatest showing of God's abundant love for us that He has; Calvary is all about love. It is where we see who we are, and what we have done, and nail it to the cross. It is where we can start over. It is the love of God the Father for us, so great, that He sacrificed His One and Only Son, Jesus Christ, in order that we might be saved from sin and an eternity in hell. (Hosea 13:14) "I will ransom them from the power of the grave; I will redeem them from death. Where, O death, are your plagues? Where, O grave is your destruction?"

When the Israelites were in bondage to the Egyptians, God sent Moses to deliver them. Pharaoh's heart was hardened, and no matter how many miracles or plagues the Lord performed through Moses, he would not let the Israelites go free. Finally, the last plague, the plague of death was set before Pharaoh. At midnight, the night of the first Passover, the Lord went throughout Egypt and every first-born male was killed. It took the death of his own son to break his heart and finally set them free. The Israelites were to smear the top and the sides of the doorframes to their houses with the blood of a year-old lamb, a lamb without defect. The lamb symbolized Jesus Christ, who was without sin, without defect. (II Corinthians 5:21) "God made Him who had no sin to be sin for us. So that in Him we might become the righteousness of God." As Jesus Christ saves us from eternal damnation, the blood of the lamb over their doors protected the Israelites from death as well. (Psalm 68:20) "Our God is a God who saves; from the Sovereign Lord comes escape from death." In doing this, the Lord provided an escape for His people. Our Almighty Father in heaven is always in control and His plans cannot be defeated. (Job 42:2) "I know that You can do all things; no plan of Yours can be thwarted." Nothing else can fill us the way He does, love us the way He loves us, or save us. It is only God, the Most High God that satisfies, saves and fills your heart and soul. It is only the God Most High that heals, protects and delivers; give yourself to Him and trust Him to take care of you and all of your needs.

As you read this name of God, pray and ask God how He has shown Himself to be the Most High God in your life. Ask how He want to show it now and in the future. Record your thoughts here.

_____

_____

_____

_____

_____

_____

_____

_____

_____

_____

_____

_____

_____

_____

5. El Olam: Everlasting God

(Isaiah 40:28) "Do you not know? Have you not heard?
The Lord is the everlasting God, the Creator of the ends
of the earth. He will not grow tired or weary, and His
understanding no one can fathom."

God is everlasting; from the beginning of time, there
was God and His word is eternal. "The grass withers and
the flowers fade, but the word of our God stands forever."
(Isaiah 40:8) El Olam means "the Everlasting God," from
an original meaning, "the God of eternity." From ancient
of Days is our God; "Yes, and from ancient days I am He.
No one can deliver out of My hand. When I act, who can
reverse it?" (Isaiah 43:13)

This means His word is everlasting, eternal, do you
speak His Word in faith, giving God glory and giving His
angels something to work with in your life on your behalf?
"Are not all angels ministering spirits sent to serve those
who will inherit salvation?" (Hebrews 1:14) Or are you
glorifying Satan and the havoc he is creating in your life by
constantly complaining about everything bad that is
happening? God's word is eternal, and it is living and
active, "For the Word of God is living and active. Sharper
than any double-edge sword, it penetrates even to dividing
soul and spirit, joints and marrow; it judges the thoughts
and attitudes of the heart." (Hebrews 4:12) How can you
give life to the words of promise in God's word if you are

not speaking them? "The Spirit gives life; the flesh counts for nothing. The words I have spoken to you are spirit and they are life." (John 6:63) According to God's word, the fruit of what you speak will come to pass. "The tongue has the power of life and death, and those who love it will eat its fruit." (Proverbs 18:21) Believe in the love and faithfulness of God and trust in His promises; He says, "I will not fail or forsake you."

It may be in a different timetable than what you "think" should happen, but you must remember that He is God and you are not! He knows the end from the beginning and He knows what it will take to answer your prayer; who He needs to use to help bring them to pass and the timetable that those specific people are on as well. Sometimes there is more involved in answering your prayers than just you and God. "For My thoughts are not your thoughts, neither are your ways My ways,' declares the Lord. 'As the heavens are higher than the earth, so are My ways higher than your ways and My thoughts than your thoughts." (Isaiah 55:8-9) If God says something in His word then by the love He has already shown in providing atonement for your sins, trust Him to bring it to pass. "So is My Word that goes out from My mouth: It will not return to Me empty; but will accomplish what I desire and achieve the purpose for which I sent it." (Isaiah 55:11)

Speak God's promises from His word and "streams of living water will flow from within" you and the Holy Spirit will give them life. How do you want to live your life? Do you want to live it in the fullness of God? God is everlasting, His Spirit is always with you and He is always faithful; He is your refuge. This world will pass away, but His love is eternal, and He always will be; "The eternal God is your refuge, and His everlasting arms are under you. He drives out the enemy before you; He cries out, 'Destroy them!'" (Deuteronomy 33:27)

God is everlasting and will love you unconditionally here on earth and into eternity. He will "never leave you nor forsake you." "For to us a child is born, to us a Son is given, and the government will be on His shoulders. And He will be called Wonderful Counselor, Mighty God, Everlasting Father, Prince of Peace." (Isaiah 9:6)

Record your thoughts on how He has shown to be everlasting, and love you unconditionally below.

_____

_____

_____

_____

_____

_____

_____

_____

_____

_____

_____

_____

_____

_____

6. El Roi: The God Who Sees

(Genesis 16:13-14) "She gave this name to the Lord who spoke to her, "You are the God who sees me;" for she said, "Have I now seen the One who sees me. That is why the well was called Beer Lahai Roi; it is still there between Kadesh and Bered."

It is truly comforting to know that no matter where you go or what you do; God always has His ever-watchful eyes on you. "For a man's ways are in full view of the Lord, and He examines all his paths." (Proverbs 5:21) So, the next time suddenly a storm arises, fear not! God is there to take care of you. "The eyes of the Lord are everywhere, keeping watch on the wicked and the good." (Proverbs 15:3) The Bible says, "The righteous will live by faith;" not fear. Fear is not from God; "For you did not receive a spirit that makes you a slave again to fear, but you received the Spirit of sonship. And by Him we cry, "*Abba*, Father." (Romans 8:15) God watches over the good and the bad; for we are all His creation; even those who reject Him. "Then God said, "Let us make man in our image, in our likeness, and let them rule over the fish of the sea and the birds of the air, over the livestock, over all the earth, and over all the creatures that move along the ground. So God created man in His own image, in the image of God He created him; male and female He created them." (Genesis 1:26-27) So yes, that means that no matter what you do or don't do, God sees. "Nothing in all creation is hidden from God's sight. Everything is uncovered and laid bare before the eyes of Him to whom we must give account." (Hebrews 4:13)

When a sudden loss happens, and the bill collectors seem to be closing in, your children are in trouble way over their head remember God and His never-ending love is always with you and watching over you. "The Lord watches over you—the Lord is your shade at your right hand; the sun will not harm you by day, nor the moon by night. The Lord will keep you from all harm—He will watch over your life; the Lord will watch over your coming and going both now and forevermore." (Psalm 121:5-8) There is never anything to fear as long as God, your heavenly Father, Creator, Savior and Friend is watching over you; fear not; God is there and He is the One who truly sees you and loves you for who you are; "I have loved you with an everlasting love; I have drawn you with loving-kindness." (Jeremiah 31:3) He knew you before you were born, what you would do and not do right; "All the days ordained for me were written in Your book before one of them came to be;" (Psalm 139:16) and He still chose to give you birth, "Praise be to the God and Father of our Lord Jesus Christ, who has blessed us in the heavenly realms with every spiritual blessing in Christ. For He chose us in Him before the creation of the world to be holy and blameless in His sight. In love He predestined us to be adopted as His sons through Jesus Christ, in accordance with His pleasure and will-- to the praise of His glorious grace, which He has freely given us in the One He loves." (Ephesians 1:3-6) He knew you completely, and He still chose to die for you "But God demonstrates His own love for us in this: While we were still sinners, Christ died for us." (Romans 5: 8)

God sees you for who you are, and nothing can separate you from Him. "My Father, who has given them to Me, is greater than all; no one can snatch them out of My Father's hand;" (John 10:29) Nothing can separate you from His love "Who shall separate us from the love of Christ? Shall trouble or hardship or persecution or famine or nakedness or danger or sword? As it is written: 'For your sake we face death all day long; we are considered a sheep to be slaughtered.' No, in all these things we are more than conquerors through Him who loved us. For I am convinced that neither death nor life, neither angels nor demons, neither the present nor the future, nor any powers, neither height nor depth, nor anything else in all creation will be able to separate us from the love of God that is in Christ Jesus our Lord." (Romans 8:35-39) Fear not; God sees you and He will "never leave you nor forsake you," Trust Him.

Look back in time, was there a time when the Lord showed up for you and left you in awe. Maybe you were in desperate need or overwhelmed in depression or heartache. Maybe a bill that needed to be paid, and you had no way to do it, but God! He showed up and showed you such overwhelming love in the situation that it left you speechless. Maybe you need it now. Record your thoughts or revelations of the Holy Spirit below.

_____

_____

_____

_____

_____

_____

_____

_____

_____

_____

_____

_____

_____

_____

7. El-Berit/Yahweh: A God of Covenant

(Judges 2:1-2) "The angel of the Lord went up from Gilgal to Bokim and said, 'I brought you up out of Egypt and led you into the land that I swore to give to your forefathers. I said, 'I will never break My covenant with you, and you shall not make a covenant with the people of this land, but you shall break down their altars."

God is a God of covenant; which means the promises He makes He is faithful to keep. "God is not a man, that He should lie, nor son of man, that He should change His mind. Does He speak and then not act? Does he promise and not fulfill?" (Numbers 23:19) Every promise He made to the Israelites, He also fulfilled and every promise that He makes to us He will fulfill as well. "The Lord is faithful to all His promises, and loving toward all He has made." (Psalm 145:13) His covenant is one that is based on His unconditional love. "I have loved you with an everlasting love; I have drawn you with loving-kindness." (Jeremiah 31:3) He promises to love us when we are sinning against Him and when we are being faithful. He loved us first when He created us, He knew us when we were in our mother's womb, He knew every good thing we would do and every bad and still chose to bring us into the world.

He loves us no matter what, and there is nothing we can do to separate us from that love. As you call on the Lord God of all creation, Yahweh, you can rest assured that He will be your God, your Father, your Savior, your Comforter, your Deliverer and your Friend no matter what you do. He will love throughout eternity; forever and ever. He does not love because of what we do, but in spite of what we do. A covenant is a binding agreement; "I will confirm My covenant between Me and you and will greatly increase your numbers." (Genesis 17:2) God is spirit and there is no flesh in Him and where people will disappoint you God never will. He who is the Glory of Israel does not lie or change His mind; for He is not a man, that He should change His mind." (I Samuel 15:29)

God gave us two confirmations of His covenant, the first being Jesus Christ and the second is His written Word; when we receive Jesus into our hearts and let His Holy Spirit, lead us, teach us, mold us, comfort us and renew our minds and hearts we will be living examples of His covenant with our eternal salvation confirmed in us through the Holy Spirit. His written Word is living and active and as we continue in it, it will be engraved on our hearts. When we pray His Word we can rest assured that our prayers will be heard and answered. "I will bow down toward your holy temple and will praise Your Name for Your love and Your faithfulness, for You have exalted above all things Your Name and Your Word." (Psalm 138:2)

He sent Jesus into the world not only to save us through His death on the cross, but to be His living covenant of love, protection and salvation for all who will receive Him. Yahweh, a God of covenant, a Covenant of Love. Is He your God? It is not too late to make Him your God. He is just a prayer away. "I, the Lord, have called you in righteousness; I will take hold of Your hand. I will keep You and will make You to be a Covenant for the people and a Light for the Gentiles, to open eyes that are blind, to free captives from prison and to release from the dungeon those who sit in darkness." (Isaiah 42:6-7)

In what ways has God showed Himself as the One true God in your life? How has He kept His covenant of love to you?

_____

_____

_____

_____

_____

_____

_____

_____

_____

_____

_____

_____

_____

_____

Powerful/Mighty God—since these next three are similar I have combined them together.

8. Elohim: Creator-Powerful God!

(Psalm 147:5) "Great is our Lord and mighty in power; His understanding has no limit." Whatever we need is ours, we just need to believe, ask in the name of Jesus and receive it by faith and it is ours.

9. El Eloah: The One God (Elohim is from Eloah)

(II Samuel 7:22) "Wherefore thou are great, Jehovah Elohim; for there is none like thee, neither is there any God beside thee, according to all that we have heard with our ears."

10. El Elohe-The Lord is Mighty

(Psalm 50:1) "The Mighty One, God, the Lord, speaks and summons the earth from the rising of the sun to the place where it sets."

There is no other God like our God; who is all-powerful, all-knowing and ever-present. "O Sovereign Lord, You have begun to show to Your servant Your greatness and Your strong hand. For what God is there in heaven or on earth who can do the deeds and mighty works you do?" (Deuteronomy 3:24) Our heavenly Father is a God of love and it is shown through His Son Jesus Christ. Instead of making us pay for our sins He sent Jesus to pay the price for us. That can be said of no one or nothing else in all creation. "The Son is the radiance of God's glory and the exact representation of His being, sustaining all things by His powerful Word. After He had provided purification for sins, He sat down at the right hand of the Majesty in heaven." (Hebrews 1:3)

Our heavenly Father is the Creator of all things and He created the heavens and the earth, the animals and the fish in the sea and the birds in the air. He still wanted a family and so He created us; He knew the beginning of our life, the in-between and the end, and still He chose to give us birth out of His never-ending, abounding love for mankind; all the while knowing each and every mistake we would make. "Yet to all who received Him, to those who believed in His name, He gave the right to become children of God—children born not of natural decent nor of human decision or a husband's will but born of God." (John 1:12-13)

Are you experiencing great trials beyond what you can bear? Then call on the mighty name of God and surrender all to His will. You are safe in His loving hands. He sees the end from the beginning and knows the best path for you to take; just as you know what is best for your children, so God knows what is best for you. "I make known the end from the beginning, from ancient times, what is still to come. I say: My purpose will stand and I will do all that I please." (Isaiah 46:10) If our God could just speak and have it happen then you can too; instead of declaring the "oh me's" and the "what about me's" and the "it will never happen" that only bring you despair, declare the promises of God that will not only bring you peace and joy but as long as you continue to stand on them, they will come true. "For the Word of God is living and active. Sharper than any double-edged sword, it penetrates even to dividing soul and spirit, joints and marrow; it judges the thoughts and attitudes of the heart." (Hebrews 4:12)

God spoke, and it came to be; the fullness of God is in His Son and the Spirit of His Son indwells in you. "For in Christ all the fullness of the Deity lives in bodily form, and you have been given fullness in Christ, who is the head over every power and authority. In Him you were also circumcised, in the putting off of the sinful nature, not with a circumcision done by the hands of men but with the circumcision done by Christ, having been buried with Him in baptism and raised with Him through your faith in the

power of God, who raised Him from the dead."
(Colossians 2:9-12) Just as God spoke and it came to be, by
the power of God that lives within you through the Holy
Spirit, all you have to do is believe and speak and keep
believing and speaking that which you have prayed for and
God will bring it to pass. "The tongue has the power of
life and death, and those who love it will eat its fruit."
(Proverbs 18:21) It is just as easy to speak out the
promises of God than those despairing "it never will"
words than only bring depression. Not only is our God a
powerful God, but He is a God who loves you just as you
are; in life people love you when you love them back or
live up to their standards; not so with God. He loves you
as you are; He has loved us first, since the beginning of all
creation. "We love because He first loved us." (I John
4:19)

Call on the wonderful name of God, your heavenly
Father who will never "fail or forsake you," sending Jesus
to die for our sins is proof of that and trust Him to bring
you out and give you victory! You have many troubles and
a lot of heartache, stop wallowing and call on the One who
will deliver you! Search the Word and speak out God's
promises for you and your loved ones! His Spirit is within
you and all you have to do is call on the power of God
within you and you will be able to stand up in your spirit
and stop laying down and letting the devil have your life,
your victory, your peace, your joy and your family! Start
believing God and His Word! Start standing on His
promises and watch your life be changed! "Your ways, O
God, are holy. What God is so great as our God? You are

the God who performs miracles; You display Your power among the peoples." (Psalm 77:13-14)

Elohim, your powerful and loving God has victory in store for you! It is promised! Believe it, pray it, speak it and wait for it to come to pass! Ask the Holy Spirit to remind you of the ways He showed up powerfully in your life in the past? How does He want to show Himself to you now?

_____

_____

_____

_____

_____

_____

_____

_____

_____

_____

_____

_____

11. Immanuel: God With Us

(Matthew 1:23) "The virgin will be with child and will give birth to a Son, and they will call Him Immanuel'— which means, "God with us."

As a child of God traveling down life's highway, no matter what you are going through, good times or bad, your Heavenly Father is always with you. "The Lord Himself goes before you and will be with you; He will never leave you nor forsake you. Do not be afraid; do not be discouraged." (Deuteronomy 31:8) Isn't that reassuring! To know that no matter what the trial is you are going through, God has already been there ahead of you, should bring you a since of relief and peace. It should help you to trust Him more. This is another way in which our Heavenly Father shows His love for us. Nothing happens here on earth without God's approval first. "The Most High is Sovereign over the kingdoms of men and gives them to anyone He wishes." (Daniel 4:25) With God and His mighty power, nothing is too difficult for Him, "With My great power and outstretched arm I made the earth and its people and the animals that are on it, and I give it to anyone I please." (Jeremiah 27:5)

We do get discouraged when the problems we are facing seem to be overwhelming. The hurt or worry we are dealing with seems to blindside us and cause us to take our eyes off Jesus. That is when discouragement and doubt will set in. Take heart, God will not let you stay that way! He loves you and will bring you back!

All you have to do is ask, He always with you, He always sees and will help you. "But if from there you seek the Lord your God, you will find Him if you look for Him with all your heart and with all your soul. When you are in distress and all these things have happened to you, then in later days you will return to the Lord your God and obey Him. For the Lord your God is a merciful God; He will not abandon or destroy you or forget the covenant with your forefathers, which He confirmed to them by oath." (Deuteronomy 4:29-31)

So out of God's overwhelming love for us, He will do whatever it takes to help us see the light and turn to Jesus Christ for our eternal salvation, to mold us and open our eyes. "God does all these things to a man-- twice, even three times-- to turn back his soul from the pit that the Light of life may shine on him." (Job 33:29-30)

Though things may get rough from time to time, know that God's ever watchful eye is on you. "The Lord watches over you-- the Lord is your shade at your right hand; the sun will not harm you by day, nor the moon by night. The Lord will keep you from all harm-- He will watch over your life; the Lord will watch over you coming and going both now and forevermore." (Psalm 121:5-8) In everything you go through, know that God is always with you, and He will lead and guide you. As long as Jesus Christ is your Lord and Savior, His Holy Spirit is always with you. "And I will ask the Father, and He will give you another Counselor to be with you forever-- the Spirit of Truth." (John 14:16)

When I feel the presence of the Lord I am more content than at any other time. Our precious Lord and Savior is always there for us. Sometimes you feel so down that you don't even feel like praying, I know this as well. But trust me, just call out His name and the rest will get easier. "The Lord is near to all who call on Him, to all who call on Him in truth." (Psalm 145:18) As you do this you will find you enjoy every moment you have with Him.

As long as you are a child of God, He will always be with you. "I will never leave you nor forsake you." (Joshua 1:5) When you go through a problem that you just can't see a way through, remember that God has already been there ahead of you and will guide you, but you have to ask. "Fear not, for I have redeemed you; I have summoned you by name; you are Mine. When you pass through the waters, I will be with you; and when you pass through the rivers, they will not sweep over you. When you walk through the fire, you will not be burned; the flames will not set you ablaze. For I am the Lord, your God, the Holy One of Israel, your Savior." (Isaiah 43:1-3)

We will go through hard times but God, Immanuel, God with us is within us through Jesus Christ; just look inside and call on His holy name and He will hear the prayers of your heart. "The kingdom of God does not come with your careful observation, nor will people say, 'Here it is,' or 'There it is,' because the kingdom of God is within you." (Luke 17:21)

God loves us so much, that He did everything possible to make sure that we would spend eternity with Him. He did that through Jesus Christ and His death on the cross; then to make sure we have what we need to live a life of victory He sent His Holy Spirit to be with us forever in our hearts. "And I pray that you, being rooted and established in love, may have power, together with all the saints, to grasp how wide and long and high and deep is the love of Christ, and know this love that surpasses knowledge--that you may be filled to the measure of all the fullness of God." (Ephesians 3:17-19)

Pray and ask the Holy Spirit to reveal to you in a personal way just how much He loves you and how He is with you, even in times that you may have felt otherwise. Record it below.

_____

_____

_____

_____

_____

_____

_____

_____

_____

_____

_____

_____

_____

_____

God of Recompense, Lord who Smites/Strikes-I am grouping together since their meaning is similar

11. Jehovah El Gmolah: The Lord God of Recompense

(Jeremiah 51:56) "A destroyer will come against Babylon; her warriors will be captured, and their bows will be broken. For the Lord is a God of retribution; He will repay in full."

12. Jehovah Nakeh: The Lord Who Smites

13. Jehovah Makkeh: The Lord Who Strikes

(Ezekiel 7:9) "I will not look on you with pity or spare you; I will repay you in accordance with your conduct and the detestable practices among you. Then you will know that it is I the Lord who strikes the blow."

Has someone wronged you? God will repay, He is the One Who Smites; He repays and brings about justice to all parties involved! Have you been deeply hurt or maybe you have been through years of hard times; always doing what is right and being faithful to the Lord and yet, your struggles do not seem to end? Fear not! There is a season for everything! "There is a time for everything, and a season for every activity under heaven." (Ecclesiastes 3:1) The Lord is faithful to all His promises and He will reward you for your faithfulness to Him. "The Lord is faithful to all His promises and loving toward all He has made." (Psalm 145:13) He is a God of love, but of justice as well and He will be faithful to reward you. "After this, the Word of the Lord came to Abram in a vision: "Do not be afraid, Abram. I am our shield, your very great reward." (Genesis 15:1) If you have been hurt deeply and someone has wronged you in a very great way, do not let a bitter root grow in your heart. It will only keep you angry and resentful and you will not just take it out on the person that hurt you if at all, you will take it out on everyone else. "You brood of vipers, how can you who are evil say anything good? For out of the overflow of the heart the mouth speaks." (Matthew 12:34) You will carry around a huge chip on your shoulder and as a child of God, being ambassadors of Christ, this should not be! Give it over to God! He will repay; He will bless your heart and heal it for letting go and forgiving and He will also bring about justice to the one that hurt you; and He can do a lot better job of it. "Do not repay anyone evil for evil. Be careful to do what is right in the eyes of everybody. If it is possible, as far as it depends on you, live at peace with everyone. Do not take revenge, my friends, but leave room for God's wrath, for it is written: 'It is Mine to avenge; I will repay, says the Lord. On the contrary: If your enemy is hungry, feed him; if he is thirsty, give him something to drink. In doing this, you will heap burning coals on his head. Do not be overcome by evil but overcome evil with good." (Romans 12:17-21)

We were enemies of Jesus while we lived in a life of sin before receiving His forgiveness, and He died for us. Out of His great love for us He forgives us; so, forgive one another. Never forget what Jesus did for you. "Praise the Lord, O my soul, and forget not all His benefits--who forgives all your sins and heals all your diseases, who redeems your life from the pit and crowns you with good things so that your youth is renewed like the eagle's." (Psalm 103:2-5)   The Lord's main goal for everyone is to save their soul and we are not to forget that; for at one time before receiving Jesus, you probably did a few things wrong yourself and hurt a few people along the way. "This is good and pleases God our Savior, who wants all men to be saved and to come to knowledge of the truth." (I Timothy 2:4)

God is a God of justice and reward; whether it is bringing justice to those that have wronged you or rewarding you for forgiving and letting go, He will fulfill all His promises. "See, the Sovereign Lord comes with power and His arm rules for Him. See, His reward is with Him and His recompense accompanies Him." (Isaiah 40:10)

When you hold on to anger and choose not to forgive, you are placing yourself in the Judges Seat and that is only meant for God. "For we know Him who said, "It is Mine to avenge; I will repay," and again, "The Lord will judge His people." (Hebrews 10:30) As long as you hold on to unforgiveness, it will also keep you at a distance from God. "For if you forgive men when they sin against you, your heavenly Father will also forgive you. But if you do not forgive men their sins, your Father will not forgive your sins." (Matthew 6:14-15)

Letting go of a past wound, will not let the guilty go unpunished; it is merely putting into the capable hands of the Creator who can bring it about in a better way than you can and possibly save their soul in the process. "The Lord is a jealous and avenging God; the Lord takes vengeance and is filled with wrath. The Lord takes vengeance on His foes and maintains His wrath against His enemies. The Lord is slow to anger and great in power; the Lord will not leave the guilty unpunished.....The Lord is good, a refuge in times of trouble. He cares for those who trust in Him, but with an overwhelming flood He will make an end of Nineveh; He will pursue His foes into darkness." (Nahum 1:1-3 & 7-8)

Let go of the hurt, the bitterness, resentment, anger and forgive! Give it over to God and He will not only make things right and repay you for the wrong done to you, but He will bless your heart with a peace that surpasses all understanding. (Isaiah 62:11-12) "The Lord has made proclamation to the ends of the earth: "Say to the Daughter of Zion, 'See, your Savior comes! See, His reward is with Him, and His recompense accompanies Him.' They will be called the Holy People, the Redeemed of the Lord and you will be called Sought After, the City No Longer Deserted." Jehovah El Gmolah: The Lord God of Recompense will come to your rescue!

Pray and ask the Holy Spirit to reveal to any anger, bitterness, resentment you may still have in your heart. If you are wanting to go deeper in Christ, to draw closer to Him, this will be a road block.

_____

_____

_____

_____

_____

_____

_____

_____

_____

_____

_____

_____

_____

_____

14. Jehovah Ezer: The Lord Our Helper

(I Samuel 7:12) "Then Samuel took a stone and set it up between Mizpah and Shen. He named it Ebenezer, saying, "Thus far has the Lord helped us."

"There is a friend who sticks closer than a brother" and His name is Jesus, our Lord. People will always fail you at one time or another; some choose too, and some will not mean to but will, but there is One who never will; Jesus. "He will never leave you nor forsake you." There are many times when dealing with the people of this world that you feel all alone. Even in your own family. If you have been born again and the people around you are not, life can be very difficult and lonely at times. I have felt this way many times, but the Lord always shows me that I am not alone. As long as Jesus Christ is your Lord and Savior, His Holy Spirit is always with you. "And I will ask the Father, and He will give you another Counselor to be with you forever-- the Spirit of Truth." (John 14:16) With the Spirit of Jesus living within your heart, you are never alone. All you have to do is call on Him and He will give you peace. "Peace I leave with you; My peace I give you. I do not give to you as the world gives. Do not let your hearts be troubled and do not be afraid." (John: 14:27)

The Israelites traveled from Egypt to the land of Canaan, and God was always with them. They sinned against Him time and time again, and God still stayed with them. That is love! He will be with you and guide you, but you are the one who must yield to Him and let Him guide you. He loves you so much; He does not want to make you love Him. But if you do, He will bless you and take care of you and supply all your needs as long as you love, trust and obey Him. "The Lord will guide you always; He will satisfy your needs in a sun-scorched land and will strengthen your frame." (Isaiah 58:11) This means even when you are going through a really rough trial and you are feeling weak and overwhelmed, trust God to strengthen you and be with you through it all. "So, we say with confidence, "The Lord is my helper, I will not be afraid. What can man do to me?" (Hebrews 13:6)

If you are in a trying time and the issues of life are overwhelming you, fear not! The Lord watches over every step you take, and He has you covered and will not let your foot slip. "The Sovereign Lord is my strength; He makes my feet like the feet of a deer, He enables me to go on the heights." (Habakkuk 3:19) God has a plan for your life and as you trust and yield to Him; He will bring it to pass watching over you every step of the way. There are trials to weed out the impurities in order to purify your heart and soul and transform your mind. There are trials to stabilize you in order for His peace to reign and rule in your life and heart and there are also trials to help bring out and perfect the gifts of the Holy Spirit. The trials that the Lord allows to come your way are only to bring you to a high place in Him; that He may use you to bless, encourage and teach others and He will help you every step of the way. "I lift up my eyes to the hills—where does my help come from? My help comes from the Lord, the Maker of heaven and earth. He will not let your foot slip—He who watches over you will not slumber; indeed, He who watches over Israel will neither slumber nor sleep. The Lord watches over you-- the Lord is your shade at your right hand; the sun will not harm you by day, nor the moon by night. The Lord will keep you from all harm-- He will watch over your life; the Lord will watch over you coming and going both now and forevermore." (Psalm 121:1-8)

What areas of your life do you need the Lord to help you in and what areas has the help He supplied truly touched your heart. Record it below.

_____

_____

_____

_____

_____

_____

_____

_____

_____

_____

_____

_____

_____

_____

15. Jehovah Gibbor –The God of War

(Isaiah 42:13) "The Lord shall go forth as a mighty man, he shall stir up jealousy like a man of war: he shall cry, yea, roar; he shall prevail against his enemies."

When the storms of life seem to hit all at once it is easy to get caught up in all the problems that come at you from all directions; fear and worry set in and despair fills your heart. Fear not! Remember that you serve a Mighty God! "Surely the arm of the Lord is not too short to save, nor His hear too dull to hear." (Isaiah 59:1) Cry out to Him; He is your heavenly Father who loves you! "Be self-controlled and alert. Your enemy the devil prowls around like a roaring lion looking for someone to devour." (I Peter 5:8) The Lord gave us His Word to give us hope and strength; something to stand firm on when trouble hits. God knew that Satan would not leave us alone to have a victorious life; He has prepared in advance the interventions you would need. "For we are God's workmanship, created in Christ Jesus to do good works, which God has prepared in advance for us to do." (Ephesians 2:10)

Trust in God, trust in His Mighty Hand! He created the world and all living things, and He can certainly save you out of your trouble! "Lift your eyes and look to the heavens: Who created all these? He who brings out the starry host one by one, and calls them each by name. Because of great power and mighty strength, not one of them is missing." (Isaiah 40:26) To look at the beauty of the world you see the Mighty Hand of the Creator. Not only this, but as powerful as God is, He loves us and cares about our burdens, and wants a relationship with us. "O Lord, what is man that you care for him, the son of man that you think of him?" (Psalm 144:3)

Isaiah 40:22 makes you see God as He is, Almighty; "He sits enthroned above the circle of the earth, and its people are like grasshoppers. He stretches out the heavens like a canopy, and spreads them out like a tent to live in." Yet, He still chose us, you and me. "But we ought always to thank God for you, brothers loved by the Lord, because from the beginning God chose you to be saved through the sanctifying work of the Spirit and through belief in the truth." (II Thessalonians 2:13)

If God has allowed something to come your way trust that it will be for your benefit. You may not see it now but when you have come through you will understand. It may be for the sake of those around you to see your faith and the way you trust God through all of your troubles and serve as a witness and a testimony to them. It may be to teach you to be stronger and help you to trust God more. Sometimes trials are the only way God has to get our attention. We do not always listen. It may be to get you to draw closer to Him or it may be to birth something new in you that can only come through the trials you are going through. "We were under great pressure, far beyond our ability to endure, so that we despaired even of life. Indeed, in our hearts we felt the sentence of death. But this happened that we might not rely on ourselves but on God." (II Corinthians 1:8-9)

Whatever the reason, trust in the One that died for you to save your soul. There is no greater love than to lay down your life for a friend and that is what He did for us.

Don't let Satan and his many attacks deceive you into doubting God's love! We serve a Mighty God and He is able to save you out of what seems to be the most impossible situations; "nothing is impossible for God." He will come to your rescue and He will pay back those who have wronged you. "The Lord your God is with you, He is Mighty to save. He will take great delight in you, He will quiet you with His love, He will rejoice over you with singing." (Zephaniah 3:17)

Pray and ask the Holy Spirit to reveal to you areas, situations or people that He wants you to release to Him to take care of, "For we know Him who said, "It is Mine to avenge; I will repay," and again, "The Lord will judge His people." (Hebrews 10:30) Record it below.

_____

_____

_____

_____

_____

_____

_____

_____

_____

_____

_____

_____

_____

_____

16. Jehovah Jireh: The Lord Provides

(Genesis 22:14) "And Abraham called the name of that place Jehovah-Jireh; as it is said at the present day. On the mount of Jehovah will be provided."

Jehovah Jireh, "The Lord Provides." God is your Creator, the very reason you have life; He provided the breath of life needed to bring you into the world. "For You created my inmost being; You knit me together in my mother's womb. I praise You because I am fearfully and wonderfully made; Your works are wonderful, I know that full well." (Psalm 139:13-14) He is your salvation—the reason you will be able to spend eternity in heaven. "For God so loved the world that He gave His One and Only Son, that whoever believes in Him shall not perish but have eternal life." (John 3:16)

He is your Father who loves and protects you and in Him you should have no fear. "For you did not receive a spirit of fear, but you received the Spirit of sonship. And by Him we cry, '*Abba, Father.*' The Spirit Himself testifies with our spirit that we are God's children. Now if we are children, then we are heirs--heirs of God and co-heirs with Christ, if indeed we share in His sufferings in order that we may also share in His glory." (Romans 8:15-17) He provides all your needs. "And my God will meet all your needs according to His glorious riches in Christ Jesus." (Philippians 4:19) He gives you strength to make it through any situation. "I can do everything through Him who gives me strength." (Philippians 4:13) The fullness of Christ lives in you and therefore whatever you need whether it is spiritual, emotional or physical; it is already provided for in Christ Jesus. Everyone has a God shaped hole in his or her heart that only God can fill. When Christ fills your heart, He makes you whole. You have His fullness and the fullness of God within you through Jesus Christ. "For in Christ all the fullness of the Deity lives in bodily form, and you have been given fullness in Christ, who is the head over every power and authority." (Colossians 2:9-10) He overcame and therefore we can too! "I have told you these things, so that in Me you may have peace. In this world you will have trouble. But take heart! I have overcome the world." (John 16:33) Whatever you need you can trust and rely on the never-ending love of God to provide it. It may not always come in the way you think it should but remember God has already been through your trial ahead of you and knows the right thing to do in the right way at the right time. "But be assured today that the Lord your

God is the One who goes across ahead of you like a devouring fire. He will destroy them; He will subdue them before you. And you will drive them out and annihilate them quickly, as the Lord has promised you." (Deuteronomy 9:3)

Not only will you be blessed, but those around you will see and glorify God and the giver He chooses to use will be blessed as well. Whatever you need, God already has a plan in place to provide it and He will sustain you through every trial and every need. "Surely God is my help; the Lord is the One who sustains me." (Psalm 54:4) Cast your cares on the Lord; He will not only take care of them, but He loves you and wants to bless you in such a way you know without a shadow of a doubt that it came from Him. "Even to your old age and gray hairs I am He, I am He who will sustain you. I have made you and I will carry you; I will sustain you and I will rescue you." (Isaiah 46:4) He provided for the burden of our sins. "Praise be the Lord, to God our Savior, who daily bears our burdens." (Psalm 68:19) He sent Jesus; so why should we ever doubt His love and desire to provide and to bless us. Place your life, your soul, your cares, your hopes and your dreams in Him; He will take care of them and provide for all your needs and will not disappoint you. "Those who hope in Me will not be disappointed." (Isaiah 49:23) God loves you and on that you can rely! He is your Jehovah Jireh—the Lord who provides! He provides for your healing for past, present and future hurts, He provides for your forgiveness for past, present and future sins and He provides for all your needs, present and future and in a greater way than you could ever imagine. "Now to Him who is able to do immeasurably more than all we ask or imagine, according to His power that is at work within us." (Ephesians 3:20) Are you in need of something? Look to your provider—Jehovah Jireh! He will provide!

Sometimes we too easily forget all the ways the Lord provides because we see the provisions every day. Provisions of a home, health, whole body, air conditioning, television and cable, electricity, phone and transportation and of course food. But to some people these are all luxuries. Ask the Lord to reveal to all the provisions He supplies you with physical, mental, emotional, spiritual, and relational. Then give Him thanks! Everyone wants to be appreciated.

_____

_____

_____

_____

_____

_____

_____

_____

_____

_____

_____

_____

_____

_____

17. Jehovah Mekadesh: The Lord Who Sanctifies You

(Hebrews 13:11-12) "The high priest carries the blood of animals into the Most Holy Place as a sin offering, but the bodies are burned outside the camp. And so, Jesus also suffered outside the city gate that He might sanctify the people with His own blood."

In life, most people want you to get cleaned up first before they will get to know you. They want you to meet their standards. That is just the way our flesh works; but there is good news! There is One who will love you just as you are, and He says come, come just as you are, I will meet you wherever you are in life. All you need to do is come! That is your Heavenly Father and our Lord Jesus Christ. He loves you with an *Agape* love; that is a love that loves regardless, unconditionally and beyond fault. "Dear friends, let us love one another, for love comes from God. Everyone who loves has been born of God and knows God. Whoever does not love does not know God, because God is love. This is how God showed His love among us: He sent His one and only Son into the world that we might live through Him. This is love: not that we loved God, but that He loved us and sent His Son as an atoning sacrifice for our sins. Dear friends, since God so loved us, we also ought to love one another. No one has ever seen God; but if we love one another, God lives in us and His love is made complete in us." (I John 4:7-12)

He loved us first and He says come, just as you are and He will transform you. "The Spirit and the bride say, "Come!' And let him who hears say, 'Come!' Whoever is thirsty, let him come; and whoever wishes, let him take the free gift of the water of life." (Revelation 22:17) You do something wrong to somebody and they get hurt and most people want to get even, but God saw all the sin in the world and instead of wanting us to pay for our sins, He sent Jesus to do that for us. That is love. "But God demonstrates His own love for us in this: While we were sinners, Christ died for us." (Romans 5:8) We are saved by grace through His blood and are made brand new! "Therefore, if anyone is in Christ, He is a new creation." (II Corinthians 5:17) He sanctifies us through His blood and we are made right with God and day by day we are transformed into the child of God He wants us to be. "May God Himself, the God of peace, sanctify you through and through. May your whole spirit, soul and body be kept blameless at the coming of our Lord Jesus Christ." (I Thessalonians 5:23)

As you continue in Christ and read the Word of God and talk to Him every day, just as you would when you are trying to get to know someone you are dating, you draw closer and closer to God. "Do not conform any longer to the pattern of this world but be transformed by the renewing of your mind." (Romans 12:2) The result is you know Him more and your love for Him grows as well, transforming your mind by the Word of God which is planted in your heart. "My son, keep My Words and store up My commands within you. Keep My commands and you will live; guard My teaching as the apple of your eye. Bind them on your fingers; write them on the tablet of your heart." Jesus is "the way and the truth and the life." (Proverbs 7:1-3)

If you will invite Him into your life you will not only have a friend for life and one that "sticks closer than a brother," but you will have a promised eternal home in heaven. He will also transform you and your life. You get a do over! How great is that! When you get a do over from Him He also wipes the slate clean and forgets forever all your past sins! The Lord washes you clean! "But you were washed, you were sanctified, you were justified in the name of the Lord Jesus Christ and by the Spirit of our God." (I Corinthians 6:11) Who on earth will do that so easily? "For I will forgive their wickedness and remember their sins no more." (Hebrews 8:12) You do not have to clean yourself up, He will do that for you.

"Sanctify them by the truth; Your word is truth. As You sent Me into the world, I have sent them into the world. For them I sanctify Myself, that they too may be truly sanctified." (John 17:17-19)

Remember the life He drew you out of? Ask the Holy Spirit to remind you of the ways He has changed you, how you have been sanctified and have been transformed from glory to glory and praise Him for that gift!

_____

_____

_____

_____

_____

_____

_____

_____

_____

_____

_____

_____

_____

18. Jehovah Perazim: The Lord My Breakthrough as a Flood

(II Samuel 5:20) "And David came to Baal-Perazim, and David defeated them there. And he said, 'The Lord has burst through my enemies before me like a bursting flood.' Therefore, the name of that place is called Baal-Perazim."

There will always be times of sowing and reaping, planting and harvesting. "As long as the earth endures, seedtime and harvest, cold and heat, summer and winter, day and night will never cease." (Genesis 8:22) In those times there will times of plenty and times in which you are hard pressed on every side. "But we were harassed at every turn—conflicts on the outside, fears within. But God, who comforts the downcast, comforted us by the coming of Titus." (II Corinthians 7:5-6) Paul endured this and walked through it in relying on God to give him the comfort that he needed to continue on his journey and service for Him. "We were under great pressure, far beyond our ability to endure, so that we despaired even of life. Indeed, in our hearts we felt the sentence of death. But this happened that we might not rely on ourselves but on God, who raises the dead." (II Corinthians 1:8-9) Paul learned to endure and to be content in any situation that came his way; knowing that the Lord would give him the strength to endure until he had completed the work assigned to him or lesson to be learned and deliver him. "For I have learned to be content whatever the circumstances. I know what it is to be in need, and I know what it is to have plenty. I have learned the secret of being content in any and every situation, whether well fed or hungry, whether living in plenty or in want. I can do everything through Him who gives me strength." (Philippians 4:11-13) There will be a day in coming that God will make all things clear to you that you need to understand and to learn through the trial you are going through. Remember that He died for you! "My command is this: Love each other as I have loved you. Greater love has no one than this that he lay down his life for his friends." (John 15:12-13)

Stop doubting and start trusting in His overwhelming, never-ending love for you. The CROSS should be all the proof you ever need. When worry sets in, remember the cross and tell yourself, "God died for me to save my soul and He will complete the work in me." God will "never leave you nor forsake you!" "Being confident of this, that He who began a good work in you will carry it on to completion until the day of Christ Jesus." (Philippians 1:6) Even if you fail along the way, God's mercy and faithfulness never ends. Praise God! "Because of the Lord's great love we are not consumed, for His compassions never fail. They are new every morning; great is Your faithfulness." (Lamentations 3:22-23) When you are first saved your heart is renewed but there is years of the world and wrong beliefs that need to be transformed; this takes time. God will do this through sermons you hear and the things you learn from reading the Bible, but He will also do it through trials. But there will come a day when finally, your new season is here! "I foretold the former things long ago, My mouth announced them and I made them known; then suddenly I acted, and they came to pass." (Isaiah 48:3)

You will get your suddenly, and you will begin to see that the times and seasons have changed in your life. "Forget the former things; do not dwell on the past. See, I am doing a new thing! Now it springs up; do you not perceive it? I am making a way in the desert and streams in the wasteland." (Isaiah 43:18-19) When God begins to move it will be like a continuous flood. When you see a flood, it is continuous and just keeps coming and that is what it will be like for you; a continuous flood of God's blessings and no one or nothing will be able to stop it or reverse it! "I, even I, am the Lord, and apart from Me there is no savior. I have revealed and saved and proclaimed—I, and not some foreign god among you. You are My witnesses,' declares the Lord, "that I am God. Yes, and from ancient days I am He. No one can deliver out of My hand. When I act, who can reverse it?" (Isaiah 43:11-13) Take heart, Jehovah Perazim; your breakthrough is coming, and He is bringing blessings with Him! Praise Him for His wonderful gift of Himself; praise Him for His wonderful gift of love! "All these blessings will come upon you and accompany you if you obey the Lord your God." (Deuteronomy 28:2)

What are you waiting for? What are you going through that seems as if time has no end for it, and has been overwhelming you? Pray and ask the Lord to speak to your heart regarding this trial; regarding His timing. Ask Him for strength and wisdom and to help you understand what He is trying to teach you. The more you are willing to learn, to obey and surrender the shorter the time between the overwhelming trial and your suddenly.

_____

_____

_____

_____

_____

_____

_____

_____

_____

_____

_____

_____

19. Jehovah Rohi (Raah): The Lord Is My Shepherd

(Psalm 23:1-3) "The Lord is my Shepherd; I shall not be in want. He makes me lie down in green pastures, He leads me beside quiet waters, He restores me soul."

Is the Lord your Shepherd? Do you let Him lead you in all your ways? Do you go to Him when making an important decision or do you move ahead without weighing the cost? When you received Jesus as Lord and Savior it was not just to be for the redemption of your soul; it was also to be the Lord of your life. Is He truly Lord of your life, over your tongue, and the way you speak to or about people. Is He the Lord over your mind, and what you think, and what you allow to penetrate your mind? Is He the Lord of your body and what you put into it and what you do with it? Don't you know that "your body is a temple of the Holy Spirit?" You cannot be a child of God and yet take part in the ways of the world. "You cannot drink the cup of the Lord and the cup of demons too; you cannot have a part in both the Lord's Table and the table of demons. Are we trying to arouse the Lord's jealousy? Are we stronger than He?" (I Corinthians 10:21-22)

Are you overwhelmed in problems; trouble has hit you in all directions; you have trouble in a relationship, bills are coming at you in every direction plus a few unexpected, and you have more bills then money coming in to pay them. Fear has set in and the peace of God seems to have dissipated. The verse above says that the Lord leads you beside quiet waters, it does not say beside turbulent waters. Let Him lead you. Get alone with Him and place your cares in His hand and listen to your heart. He will speak to your heart and guide you and tell you what to do. "Cast your cares on the Lord and He will sustain you; He will never let the righteous fall." (Psalm 55:22) Faith is what moves Him; it lets Him know that you believe in Him and you know that He loves you and you trust Him to take care of you and deliver you; "without faith it is impossible to please Him." In coming to the Promised Land the Israelites had to cross the Jordan River and it was at a time of year when the waters were flowing heavily. Just like the problems that are hitting you right now.

You feel overwhelmed, as if a flood has suddenly overtaken you. The Lord has not given you a "spirit that makes you a slave again to fear, but you received the Spirit of sonship. And by Him we cry, '*Abba*,' Father." The Lord died for you! "Greater love has no one than this, that he lay down his life for his friends." So why do you fear, why do you doubt? Fear tells you that He will not come through for you and He is telling you all through His Word that He loves you, He died for you and He will deliver and protect you! Fear will only immobilize you and keep you at the mountain of trouble longer than you want to stay! It is time to move!

It is time to step in the water of faith and wait in expectation for God to move on your behalf to deliver you! Step into the water and the flow will stop. Just as He told the Israelites about to cross the Jordan at flood season; "Now the Jordan is at flood stage all during harvest. Yet as soon as the priests who carried the ark reached the Jordan and their feet touched the water's edge, the water from upstream stopped flowing." (Joshua 3:15-16) Step into the water of faith and watch and see what God will do for you! "Now to Him who is able to do immeasurably more than all we ask or imagine, according to His power that is at work within us, to Him be glory in the church and in Christ Jesus throughout all generations, for ever and ever! Amen." (Ephesians 3:20-21)

The Lord is your Shepherd who cares for you; trust Him to lead you safely through your trials into your Promised Land. What areas do you need to step out and trust God more in? Ask the Holy Spirit to reveal them to you.

_____

_____

_____

_____

_____

_____

_____

_____

_____

_____

_____

_____

_____

_____

_____

20. Jehovah Rophe/Rapha: The Lord Heals

(Exodus 15:26) "I am the Lord who heals you."

The Lord Almighty heals. He is the healer of broken bodies, broken spirits and broken relationships. First and foremost, He is the healer of your lost soul; through the death and resurrection of Jesus Christ our souls are forever healed, saved! That is only possible by believing in who He is and what He did for you and receiving Him into your heart. "That if you confess with your mouth, 'Jesus is Lord," and believe in your heart that God raised Him from the dead, you will be saved. For it is with your heart that you believe and are justified, and it is with your mouth that you confess and are saved." (Romans 10:9-10)

He is the Lord who heals your heart; your emotions.

"The Spirit of the Sovereign Lord is on Me, because the Lord has anointed Me to preach good news to the poor. He has sent Me to bind up the brokenhearted, to proclaim freedom for the captives and release from darkness for the prisoners, to proclaim the year of the Lord's favor and the day of vengeance of our God, to comfort all who mourn, and provide for those who grieve in Zion—to bestow on them a crown of beauty instead of ashes, the oil of gladness instead of mourning and a garment of praise instead of a spirit of despair. They will be called oaks of righteousness, a planting of the Lord for the display of His splendor." (Isaiah 61:1-3)

He is the Lord who heals your mind; He changes wrong thinking into right. "Do not conform any longer to the pattern of this world, but be transformed by the renewing of your mind. Then you will be able to test and approve what God's will is—His good, pleasing and perfect will." (Romans 12:2) He straightens the path beneath you from the wrong decisions you made with a wrong mindset. "Trust in the Lord with all your heart and lean not on your own understanding; in all your ways acknowledge Him, and He will make your paths straight." (Proverbs 3:5-6) He makes your crooked paths straight "Every valley shall be filled in, every mountain and hill made low. The crooked roads shall become straight, the rough ways smooth." . (Luke 3:5)

Do you have an illness; call on the name of Jesus; He is the Lord who heals. "I have seen his ways, but I will heal him; I will guide him and restore comfort to him, creating praise on the lips of the mourners in Israel. Peace, peace,

to those far and near,' says the Lord. 'And I will heal them."
(Isaiah 57:18-19) Call on His name for He is the Lord who
heals; where there is poverty, He will restore. "The
blessing of the Lord brings wealth, and He adds no trouble
to it." (Proverbs 10:22)

The Lord will restore; He is the Repairer of Broken
Walls; your broken families and relationships. "The Lord
will guide you always; He will satisfy your needs in a sun-
scorched land and will strengthen your frame. Your people
will rebuild the ancient ruins and will raise up the age-old
foundations; you will be called Repairer of Broken Walls,
Restorer of Streets with Dwellings." (Isaiah 58:11-12) The
Lord restores and gives life and He is calling you to lean on
Him. What He promises in His Word He will do and He
will not forsake them. Where there is darkness in your
life; the Lord heals and turns the darkness to light. "I will
lead the blind by ways they have not known, along
unfamiliar paths I will guide them; I will turn the darkness
into light before them and make the rough places smooth.
These are the things I will do; I will not forsake them."
(Isaiah 42:16)

He will give you strength to endure and peace to
comfort your heart. "The Lord gives strength to His
people; the Lord blesses His people with peace." (Psalm
29:11) If the healing you need involves many areas of your
life and you need total deliverance, just trust in His
unconditional love and give Him time to answer.

"The Spirit of the Lord is on Me, because He has
anointed Me to preach good news to the poor. He has
sent Me to proclaim freedom for the prisoners and
recovery of sight for the blind, to release the oppressed, to
proclaim the year of the Lord's favor." (Luke 4:18-19)

What do you need healing for, your mind, your heart, your body, or maybe your spirit? You know there is something missing in your walk in Christ but just do not know what it is, ask! Pray and ask the Holy Spirit to reveal it to you

_____

_____

_____

_____

_____

_____

_____

_____

_____

_____

_____

_____

_____

21. Jehovah Sabbaoth: The Lord of Hosts

(Amos 4:13) "For behold, He who forms mountains and creates the wind and declares to man what are His thoughts, He who makes dawn into darkness and treads on the high places of the earth, the Lord God of Hosts is His name."

Rejoice! For you have the Lord God of heaven, creator of heaven and earth and all that dwell in it as your heavenly Father. "The earth is the Lord's and everything in it, the world and all who live in it; for He founded it upon the seas and established it upon the waters." (Psalm 24:1-2) He is your Father, your Savior and deliverer, your helper, healer and provider! Rejoice! You may be experiencing a battle at the moment that is more than you can bear, well, fear not, God will come to save you! "Be strong, do not fear; your God will come, He will come with vengeance; with divine retribution He will come to save you." (Isaiah 35:4) Trust Him, love and praise Him and be patient with Him to work out your deliverance and He will come just as He promises! "Wait for the Lord; be strong and take heart and wait on the Lord." (Psalm 27:14) If you read in the Old Testament the battles that the Israelites had to fight on the way to the Promised Land, you will see that as long as the Lord was with them, they won the battle every time and He is no respecter of persons; He will do the same for you. "For everyone born of God overcomes the world. This is the victory that has overcome the world, even our faith." (I John 5:4) Do you have a whirlwind of problems right now that only God can solve? Well, take them to Him and let Him! Give control back over to Him! When the Israelites were fighting the Amalekites, they were winning as long as Moses' hands were raised. In other words, as long as you keep God first, as long as you keep worshipping and praising Him and trusting Him to deliver you, you will win every time!

"So we say with confidence, "The Lord is my helper, I will not be afraid. What can man do to me?" (Hebrews 13:6) The Creator of all things is your friend and your Father, and He loves you and watches over you and there is nothing in this world that can succeed against Him. "What, then, shall we say in response to this? If God is for us, who can be against us?" (Romans 8:31) Do you have financial trouble, a job loss, in need of food? The Lord will sustain you, He is your Jehovah Jireh; your Provider. "Cast all your cares on the Lord and He will sustain you, He will never let the righteous fall." (Psalm 55:22) "Even to your old age and gray hairs I am He, I am He who will sustain you. I have made you and I will carry you; I will sustain you and I will rescue you." (Isaiah 46:4) Through every burden you have you know that you can go to the Lord with confidence in knowing that He will help you. What an awesome show of love! God promises to take care of your needs, all you have to do is love, trust and obey Him. His work seems to be a whole lot harder, because, talking from experience; we sure can make a mess out of things. "Praise be to the Lord, to God our Savior, who daily bears our burdens." (Psalm 68:19) Do you have people coming against you, relationships falling apart and legal issues that only God can solve? He wants to and He will get the glory that will also be a witness to those around you which will not only touch your heart, but theirs as well. God will level every mountain in your life; trust Him and give Him time to work it out; then watch and see just how He will come to your rescue! "So, he said to me, 'this is the word of the Lord to Zerubbabel: 'Not by might nor by power, but by My Spirit,' says the Lord Almighty. What are you, O mighty mountain? Before Zerubbabel you will become level ground. Then he will bring out the capstone to shouts of 'God bless it! God bless it!'" (Zechariah 4:6-7)

"Thus, says Jehovah the King of Israel and his Redeemer, the Lord of hosts: 'I am the first and I am the last and there is no God besides Me." (Isaiah 44:6)

Problems overwhelming you? Take them to God and you will be delivered and gain victory over everything! "With God we will gain the victory and He will trample down our enemies." (Psalm 60:12) Pray and ask the Holy Spirit to reveal to you His heart regarding the mountains in your life.

_____

_____

_____

_____

_____

_____

_____

_____

_____

_____

_____

_____

_____

_____

_____

22. Jehovah Shalom: The Lord is Your Peace

(Judges 6:24) "Then Gideon built an altar there unto the Lord and called it Jehovah Shalom; unto this day it is yet in Ophrah of the Abiezrites."

Are you surrounded by overwhelming circumstances? You have trouble at home, trouble on your job, bills coming out of nowhere, and more of them then money in your paycheck to cover them. You can have peace in the middle of the storm. The Spirit of our Lord is within you and He says, "You dear children, are from God and have overcome them, because the One who is in you is greater than the one who is in the world." (I John 4:4) Jesus went through trials and testing and was made in human form so He could fully understand us and the emotions we experience when we go through hardships. "For this reason He had to be made like His brothers in every way, in order that He might become a merciful and faithful High Priest in service to God, and that He might make atonement for the sins of the people. Because He Himself suffered when He was tempted, He is able to help those who are being tempted." (Hebrews 2:17-18) You can have peace in the storm if your eyes are on the greatness of your God instead of the storm.

The answer to your trials and the wisdom and strength you need to continue rests in the storm. "A furious squall came up, and the waves broke over the boat, so that it was nearly swamped. Jesus was in the stern, sleeping on a cushion." (Mark 4:37-38) God is greater than the storms of life that we go through. "How great is God—beyond our understanding! The number of His years is past finding out." (Job 36:26) When you are overwhelmed and are tempted to cave in to despair and depression and lose hope, just get alone with God! Even Jesus needed to withdraw to a solitary place; a place to get alone and pray! So, how much more so do we; He was all God and all flesh. We are all flesh with His Spirit living within us. "Very early in the morning, while it was still dark, Jesus got up, left the house and went off to a solitary place, where He prayed." (Mark 1:35) While it was dark, Jesus went to pray.

We need communion with God in good times when the light of day is shining on every part of our life and in our darkest moments. God does not want to just be your "911" God! He is your God, your Creator and your Savior, but He is also your Father who loves you. He wants to know the big things going on in your life and the small ones. He wants to know your big desires and your small ones. He created us to be His family. Do you only call your mom or dad or friends when you need something? Or, do you call them just to talk as well? God wants sincere devotion; He wants to be loved for who He is and not just what He can do for you. "God is spirit, and His worshipers must worship in spirit and in truth." (John 4:24) When come to a place in your life where you know beyond a shadow of a doubt that God loves you even when darkness surrounds you and you do not question but can say as Mary did, "I am the Lord's servant,' Mary answered. 'May it be to me as you have said;" (Luke 1:38) then you can know that you have spiritually matured and your relationship with God is sincere; that you are a friend of God.

"And the Scripture was fulfilled that says, 'Abraham believed God, and it was credited to him as righteousness,' and he was called God's friend." (James 2:23) When you feel overwhelmed just get alone with God and let Him strengthen you again. "The Lord gives strength to His people; the Lord blesses His people with peace." (Psalm 29:11) If He is allowing something in your life it is only to teach you something, to grow you in a certain area or to draw impurities out of you. The One who died for you will only allow things to come your way if it is for your good. "And we know that in all things God works for the good of those who love Him, who have been called according to His purpose." (Romans 8:28)

Get alone with God and talk to Him, tell Him what is going on in your life; pray to Him and worship Him and let Him strengthen you. Humble yourselves unto Him and trust Him and soon enough He will deliver you. Let His peace consume you in the middle of the storm and strengthen you to carry on until He brings you out. "Be self-controlled and alert. Your enemy the devil prowls around like a roaring lion looking for someone to devour. Resist him, standing firm in the faith, because you know that your brothers throughout the world are undergoing the same kind of sufferings. And the God of all grace, who called you to His eternal glory in Christ, after you have suffered a little while, will Himself restore you and make you strong, firm and steadfast. To Him be the power for ever and ever. Amen." **(I Peter 5:8-11)** What area in your life do you need peace? A relationship, your job, finances, emotional problems?

Go to God in prayer and allow the Holy Spirit to speak to your heart regarding your situation. Record it below.

_____

_____

_____

_____

_____

_____

_____

_____

_____

_____

_____

_____

_____

_____

23. Jehovah Shammah: The Lord is There/Present

(Zechariah 2:10) "Sing for joy and be glad, O daughter of Zion; for behold I am coming, and I will dwell in your midst, 'declares the Lord."

Are you overwhelmed; are you in the midst of a storm? Then take comfort in knowing that the Lord God Almighty, Jehovah Shammah is there! You cannot see the wind, but you can feel and see its effects. You cannot see your Almighty Father in Heaven, but you can feel His presence and see the effect of having the Holy Spirit living within you. Your heart is at rest and you feel His peace. "Peace I leave with you; My peace I give you. I do not give to you as the world gives. Do not let your hearts be troubled and do not be afraid." (John 14:27) The Lord God has said, "I will never leave you nor forsake you." God is all Spirit and all love and truth. The flesh is weak and there is no flesh in Him. When man will fail you God will not. "The Lord is faithful to all His promises and loving toward all He has made." (Psalm 145:13) Who in all the world would innocently give their life in exchange for the sins of many? Our God did; He sent His only Son to pay the price for our sins. When you need someone to be there for you; God always will. Are you sad and lonely; the Lord is there. "A man of many companions may come to ruin, but there is a friend who sticks closer than a brother." (Proverbs 18:24)

Are you brokenhearted; the Lord is there to comfort you. "The Lord is close to the brokenhearted and saves those who are crushed in spirit." (Psalm 34:18) Are you sick in your body; the Lord is there. "Praise the Lord, O my soul; all my inmost being, praise His holy name. Praise the Lord, O my soul, and forget not all His benefits—who forgives all your sins and heals all your diseases, who redeems your life from the pit and crowns you with love and compassion, who satisfies your desires with good things so that your youth is renewed like the eagle's." (Psalm 103:1-5) Have you lost someone you love; are you depressed; the Lord is there. "The Spirit of the Sovereign Lord is on Me, because the Lord has anointed Me to preach good news to the poor. He has sent Me to bind up the brokenhearted, to proclaim freedom for the captives and release from darkness for the prisoners, to proclaim the year of the Lord's favor and the day of vengeance of our God, to comfort all who mourn, and provide for those who grieve in Zion—to bestow on them a crown of beauty instead of ashes, the oil of gladness instead of mourning, and a garment of praise instead of a spirit of despair. They will be called oaks of righteousness, a planting of the Lord for the display of His splendor." (Isaiah 61:1-3)

Are you in need; the Lord is there. "And my God will meet all your needs according to His glorious riches in Christ Jesus." (Philippians 4:19) Are you in need of someone to love you, who will never fail you, leave you or hurt you? Someone who will love you just as you are no matter how many times you mess up or make mistakes; someone who will always love you no matter what? The Lord is there; call to Him, Jehovah Shammah. "Who shall separate us from the love of Christ? Shall trouble or hardship or persecution or famine or nakedness or danger or sword? As it is written: 'For your sake we face death all day long; we are considered a sheep to be slaughtered.' No, in all these things we are more than conquerors through Him who loved us. For I am convinced that neither death nor life, neither angels nor demons, neither the present nor the future, nor any powers, neither height nor depth, nor anything else in all creation will be able to separate us from the love of God that is in Christ Jesus our Lord." (Romans 8:35-39)

(Ezekiel 48:35) "And the name of the city from that time on will be: the Lord is there." What is it that you need, what area do you just need God to step in and take over? Pour out your heart to Him below.

_____

_____

_____

_____

_____

_____

_____

_____

_____

_____

_____

_____

_____

_____

24. Jehovah Tsidkenu: The Lord is our Righteousness

(Jeremiah23:5-6) "The days are coming,' declares the Lord, 'when I will raise up to David a righteous Branch, a King who will reign wisely and do what is just and right in the land. In His days Judah will be saved and Israel will live in safety. This is the name by which He will be called: The Lord Our Righteousness."

There is no greater gift than the gift of salvation, the gift of eternal salvation. "Greater love has no one than this that he lay down his life for his friends." (John 15:13) Salvation is a gift; it is the overwhelming love of our Creator who saw that on our own, we could not live up to His holy standards and decided to work out our salvation Himself. How can anyone doubt His love? "He saw that there was no one, He was appalled that there was no one to intervene; so His own arm worked salvation for Him, and His own righteousness sustained Him. He put on the righteousness as His breastplate, and the helmet of salvation on His head; He put on the garments of vengeance and wrapped Himself in zeal as in a cloak." (Isaiah 59:16-17) Salvation is the gift and grace of God, but it is a gift in which we need to ask for; God will not force Himself on anyone. The Holy Spirit is a gentleman. "That if you confess with your mouth, 'Jesus is Lord,' and believe in your heart that God raised Him from the dead, you will be saved. For it is with your heart that you believe and are justified, and it is with your mouth that you confess and are saved." (Romans 10:9-10) As we are now a new creation in Christ, we are to be holy as He is holy. Whenever you are pressured to be a certain way it becomes hard to live up to the standard of what was placed on you. That is something that is natural to everyone because we are all flesh and the flesh is weak. We all fall and make mistakes. So, the grace of God was extended to us to help us to become the righteousness of God's Holy standards. The gift of salvation is an awesome gift in itself, but to add to that gift, God in His unselfish abounding love for us gave us another gift, the gift of righteousness through Jesus Christ. Through Him we are made holy and righteous! What an awesome gift! It is like someone telling you that a bill you owe and is so much that you could never get it paid off on your own has been paid in full! That would be and enormous weight off of your shoulders. Jesus did that for us. "And such were some of you; but you have been washed, you have been made holy, you have been given righteousness in the Name of the Lord Jesus Christ and in the Spirit of our God." (I Corinthians 6:11)

He took the weight of sin off of our shoulders and gave us the ability to live a righteous holy life through the blood He shed on the cross. "He Himself bore our sins in His body on the tree, so that we might die to sins and live for righteousness; by His wounds you have been healed." (I Peter 2:24) He became the atonement for our sins and through receiving His Holy Spirit we are made righteous in the sight of God. A gift, free and all you have to do is believe and receive! God created us for His glory and to be His children. "Yet to all who received Him, to those who believed in His name, He gave the right to become children of God." (John 1:12)

In heaven there is no sin, no pain, no heartache, no tears, no illness, and no death. There is no evil. God is good and God is love. "Dear friends, let us love one another, for love comes from God. Everyone who loves has been born of God and knows God. Whoever does not love does not know God, because God is love. This is how God showed His love among us: He sent His One and Only Son into the world that we might live through Him. This is love: not that we loved God, but that He loved us and sent His Son as an atoning sacrifice for our sins." (I John 4: 7-10)

Love and evil cannot co-exist. That is why God has Holy Standards to live by; but in His overwhelming love for us, He knew by the weakness of our flesh that we could not live up to those standards and if He left it to us, He would not have us with Him in heaven. We are all flesh and are all weak; not one person would make it. "All of us have become like one who is unclean, and all our righteous acts are like filthy rags." (Isaiah 64:6) Out of His overwhelming love for us, He became a man through Jesus Christ His One and Only Son. He sent Him to die for our sins and pay the price for us. A price too high for us to pay and through His Holy Spirit within us, make is possible for us to live holy and righteous lives. The Law was given only to make us aware of what sin is and to help us to see that we cannot do it on our own; that we might call upon God and His Son. Through Jesus we are made righteous; He is our Righteousness! "Now we know that whatever the law says, it says to those who are under the law, so that every mouth may be silenced and the whole world held accountable to God. Therefore no one will be declared righteous in his own sight by observing the law; rather, through the law we become conscious of sin. But now righteousness from God, apart from the law, has been made known, to which the Law and the Prophets testify. This righteousness from God comes through faith in Jesus Christ to all who believe. There is no difference, for all have sinned and fall short of the glory of God, and are justified freely by His grace through the redemption that came by Christ Jesus. God presented Him as a sacrifice of atonement, through faith in His blood. He did this to demonstrate His justice, because in His forbearance he had left the sins committed beforehand unpunished--He did it to demonstrate His justice at the present time, so as to be just and the One who justifies those who have faith in Jesus." (Romans 3:19-26)

Is He your righteousness? Have you made Him Lord of your life? You cannot draw any closer to Him until you make that confession? Maybe you have backslidden, being made right is just a prayer away.   Ask the Holy Spirit to reveal any sin you have not confessed, then take that to Him. Ask for forgiveness. Record your prayers and thoughts below.

_____

_____

_____

_____

_____

_____

_____

_____

_____

_____

_____

_____

_____

25. Jehovah-Nissi: The Lord is My Banner

(Exodus 17:15-16) "Moses built an altar and called it the Lord is my Banner. He said, 'For hands were lifted up to the throne of the Lord. The Lord will be at war against the Amalekites from generation to generation."

The word "banner" in the dictionary means flag. The United States flag is a symbol of our freedom. It is a symbol that we are states united into one country; a country governed within itself and not governed by any other country. The Lord is our "Banner" and He is a symbol of our freedom; freedom from the bondage of sin and freedom from any stronghold Satan tries to attack you with and lead you back into bondage. He is a symbol of our victory and power that we have in Him. "Now if we died with Christ, we believe that we will also live with Him. For we know that since Christ was raised from the dead, He cannot die again; death no longer has mastery over Him. The death He died, He died to sin once for all; but the life He lives, He lives to God. In the same way, count yourselves dead to sin but alive to God in Christ Jesus. Therefore, do not let sin reign in your mortal body so that you obey its evil desires. Do not offer the parts of your body to sin, as instruments of wickedness, but rather offer yourselves to God, as those who have been brought from death to life; and offer the parts of your body to Him as instruments of righteousness. For sin shall not be your master, because you are not under law, but under grace." (Romans 6:8-14)

Not only is Jesus Christ a symbol of our freedom, but our strength as well. When we need strength, help in getting through a trial, healing or other necessities of life, He is our banner and the One that we run to! "The name of the Lord is a strong tower; the righteous run to it and are safe." (Proverbs 18:10) Is life overwhelming you? Do you have troubles hitting you in all directions and you do not know what to do? Then run to the Lord; run to Him in prayer and in His Word. "The Lord is my light and my salvation—whom shall I fear? The Lord is the stronghold of my life—of whom shall I be afraid?" (Psalm 27:1) In II Chronicles 20, King Jehosephat was facing 3 vast armies and he did not know what to do. So, he fasted and prayed. The Lord told him that the battle belongs to the Lord and to face your enemy with praise! This will confuse them. When Satan is throwing things to send you into despair and fear and you face the problem with trust and praise to God he will not know what to do. It will confuse him. That is what happened, they fought against each other in total confusion and the Israelites won!

When the Israelites were fighting the Amalekites, they were winning as long as Moses was holding up his hands. Holding them up in praise! When he grew tired they put a rock under him. That rock is a symbol of Jesus, our Rock and our Redeemer! "The Lord upholds all those who fall and lifts up all who are bowed down." (Psalm 145:14) The Lord will give you wisdom and a new found strength and hope to help you endure. "May the God of hope fill you with all joy and peace as you trust in Him, so that you may overflow with hope by the power of the Holy Spirit." (Romans 15:13) He is your strength and encouragement whenever you need it. Just call on His name and He will be there to rescue you. "I will make you a wall to this people, a fortified wall of bronze; they will fight against you but will not overcome you, for I am with you to rescue and save you, 'declares the Lord." (Jeremiah 15:20) Bronze is a symbol of judgment; so in making you a wall of bronze to your enemies the Lord is saying that they will run into judgment as well for attacking you. So, fear not! The Lord is with you and He "will not leave or forsake you." Run to the Lord, your Banner; Jehovah-Nissi and be safe!

"Do not fret because of evil men or be envious of those who do wrong; for like the grass they will soon wither, like green plants they will soon die away. Trust in the Lord and do good; dwell in the land and enjoy safe pasture. Delight yourself in the Lord and He will give you the desires of your heart. Commit your way to the Lord; trust in Him and He will do this: He will make your righteousness shine like the dawn, the justice of your cause like the noonday sun." (Psalm 37:1-6)

In Christ you are a winner, the victory is already yours! Be patient and trust God, keep persevering and obeying and it will manifest! (Psalm 60:12) "With God we will gain the victory, and He will trample down our enemies."

Where do you need victory? Pray to Him and ask for His help. Pray and ask for a fresh revelation to give you hope to continue. Record it below.

_____

_____

_____

_____

_____

_____

_____

_____

_____

_____

_____

_____

_____

_____

26. El Bethel: The God of the House of God

(Genesis 35:7) "He built an altar there, and called the place El-bethel because there God had revealed Himself to him when he fled from his brother."

"But I, by Your great mercy, will come into your house; in reverence will I bow down toward Your holy temple." (Psalm 5:7) Why do you come to church? Is it because of duty? You think it is part of being a Christian and you need to go? God is omnipresent; His Spirit is everywhere, and we can worship Him and talk to Him wherever we are so, why do we come to church? Part of going to church is by God's command to keep the Sabbath day Holy. It is in reverence to Him. He created the world in six days and on the seventh He rested and for all that He is, Creator we should worship Him. The Sabbath day was originally on Saturday, but in Acts 20:7 they began meeting on Sunday, "On the first day of the week, we came together to break bread." They did this in remembrance of Jesus who rose from the dead on Sunday.

We come to church to receive a Word from God as well; it may be a word of encouragement, a word of correction or a word to guide you in a certain direction. But, the heart of why we should always come to church is to WORSHIP GOD! David, in II Samuel 20 was coming back to the City of David. He was returning home from recovering the Ark of God from the house of Obed-Edom. He came rejoicing and took off his kingly robes and danced and sang praises to God. This means that he got rid of all his pride and who he was and humbled himself before the Lord and worshipped Him straight from His heart. This is why we go to church; to worship the Lord with gladness! "Worship the Lord with gladness; come before Him with joyful songs." (Psalm 100:2)

We are saved, and we have an eternal home in heaven that awaits us; we have a reason to praise Him! David disrobed and praised God and we should do the same. We need to rid ourselves of our own agenda and of the way we may think the service should be run, or the way we may think someone needs to dress. Leave your opinions and your judgmental attitudes behind; they will only stunt your spiritual growth. Enter into His courts with a joyful song in your heart full of His love! "Enter His gates with thanksgiving and His courts with praise; give thanks to Him and praise His name." (Psalm 100:4)

Remember where you came from before you were saved; remember the times you did not have much money, and could not afford to buy clothes and leave the judgmental, legalistic, religious attitudes at the door! Put on a new self in Christ full of love and devotion to God. "You were taught, with regard to your former way of life, to put off your old self, which is being corrupted by its deceitful desires; to be made new in the attitude of your minds; and to put on the new self, created to be like God in true righteousness and holiness." Come into the house of God with a heart ready to praise Him! (Ephesians 4:22-24)

"God is spirit, and His worshipers must worship Him in spirit and in truth." (John 4:24) Is your heart in the right place when you come into the house of God? Do you come ready to worship and to receive a word from Him? God is love and if His Holy Spirit is truly within you; walking in love everyday and the desire to worship God should be who you are; is it? "Praise the Lord, O my soul, and forget not all His benefits—who forgives all your sins and heals all your diseases, who redeems your life from the pit and crowns you with good things so that your youth is renewed like the eagle's." (Psalm 103:2-5) You are also the house, the temple of God and so is the home that you live in, do you live, love and act in a way that displays that?

"By His power God raised the Lord from the dead, and He will raise us also. Do you not know that your bodies are members of Christ himself? Shall I then take the members of Christ and unite them with a prostitute? Never! Do you not know that he who unites himself with a prostitute is one with her in body? For it is said, "The two will become one flesh." But whoever is united with the Lord is one with him in spirit. Flee from sexual immorality. All other sins a person commits are outside the body, but whoever sins sexually, sins against their own body. Do you not know that your bodies are temples of the Holy Spirit, who is in you, whom you have received from God? You are not your own; you were bought at a price. Therefore, honor God with your bodies." (I Corinthians 6:14-20)

Are there areas in your life or your worship that has been lacking in your honor of God? Pray and ask the Holy Spirit to reveal those areas. What about recent revelations, changes? Record those as well praising Him for making that known.

_____

_____

_____

_____

_____

_____

_____

_____

_____

_____

_____

_____

7. Elohim Chaseddi: The God of My Mercy

(Psalm 59:10) "My God (Elohim) in His lovingkindness will meet me; God will let me look triumphantly upon my foes."

"Because of the Lord's great love we are not consumed, for His compassions never fail. They are new every morning; great is Your faithfulness." (Lamentations 3:22-23) You messed up yesterday; you lost your temper or you said something when you should have kept quiet or you did something you shouldn't have or maybe you went back to some of your old ways. Fear not! You can begin again! The best part of being a child of God is we always get a do-over! Just admit to God that you did wrong; repent, and then let it go! "If we claim to be without sin, we deceive ourselves and the truth is not in us. If we confess our sins, He is faithful and just and will forgive us our sins and purify us from all unrighteousness." (I John 1:8-9) Repent and forgive yourself; let it go! God already did the moment you asked for forgiveness! Isn't He wonderful! "For I will forgive their wickedness and will remember their sins no more." (Hebrews 8:12)

Everything that we do in a life apart from God (as sinners), upon asking for forgiveness, our sins are gone, wiped out! That is an awesome show of love, mercy and compassion! For great is God's love and mercy towards us! In the Book of II Kings, Naaman, commander of the king of Aram's army had leprosy. He went to Elisha to heal him. He told him to go and wash himself in the Jordan River seven times. Naaman went away angry. He assumed that Elisha would do something great. He almost missed out on his healing. His servant asked him if he had told him to do something great would he not have done it so, why not this? Naaman humbled himself and did as Elisha had told him. He was cured and was very grateful! Not just for the healing, but more for the mercy that was shown. He had gone away with an attitude, but when he humbled himself and did as he was told, he was still healed. The leprosy here is a symbol of sin. The way he was healed, just by washing himself in the Jordan seven times, and how easy it was, is a symbol of how easy it really is to receive forgiveness of your sins and to be saved. The washing in the Jordan is a symbol of how we are cleansed by the blood of Jesus and our sins are forgiven. Jesus is our 'living water.' "If anyone is thirsty, let him come to Me and drink. Whoever believes in Me, as the Scripture has said, streams of living water will flow from within him." (John 7:38)

No one should ever doubt God's love. "Greater love has no one than this that he lay down his life for his friends." (John 15:13) Satan tries to keep our eyes on our circumstances and make us doubt. But always remember how He made it possible to forgive you and how easy He makes it to receive. We are the ones who make it hard.

"Therefore, as God's chosen people, holy and dearly loved, clothe yourselves with compassion, kindness, humility, gentleness and patience. Bear with each other and forgive whatever grievances you may have against one another. Forgive as the Lord forgave you. And over all these virtues put on love, which binds them all together in perfect unity." (Colossians 3:12-14) For that is what forgiveness is all about; Love. Forgive yourself and receive God's forgiveness. Wallowing in the guilt of what you did is from Satan and will only keep you down and stunt your spiritual growth; receive God's forgiveness and as Jesus told the lame man, "pick up your mat and walk." In other words, don't get comfortable in self-pity and guilt; you are forgiven! God's has new mercies every morning; grab them and go on! How great is the Father's love! "How great is the love the Father has lavished on us, that we should be called children of God!" (I John 3:1)

By God's great mercy we are not only the best gift, salvation, and a promised home in eternity, but also new mercies every morning! We all need that, we are all human and weak. In Him we are made strong, and by His mercy we have the Holy Spirit dwelling within us to give us that strength. Give Him praise for all the mercies He has shown you. Record them below.

_____

_____

_____

_____

_____

_____

_____

_____

_____

_____

_____

_____

_____

_____

28. El Emunah: The Faithful God

(Deuteronomy 7:9) "Know therefore that the Lord your God is God; He is the faithful God, keeping His covenant of love to a thousand generations of those who love Him and keep His commandments."

"Praise the Lord, all you nations; extol Him, all you peoples. For great is His love toward us, and the faithfulness of the Lord endures forever." (Psalm 117:1-2) God in His faithfulness never changes. His love is constant. He doesn't move; we do. "Jesus Christ is the same yesterday and today and forever." (Hebrews 13:8) God loves us through all our good times and bad. He loves us when we are rebelling against Him and when we submit to Him. He is very patient with us. "He is patient with you, not wanting anyone to perish, but everyone to come to repentance." (II Peter 3: 9) God is All Powerful, All Knowing, and Sovereign over all things, and yet He is still gentle and patient with us. Even when we mess up and make mistakes He still loves us. He is always there with open arms waiting for us to hear the sweet whispers of His convictions pointing us in the right direction and telling us what we are doing wrong. He is always there waiting for us to say, "Please forgive me" or to go in the direction He is trying to lead us.

God's faithfulness is another way in which He shows His love for us. Even when we are not, God is still faithful! Praise God! For He truly is wonderful! "If we are faithless, He will remain faithful, for He cannot disown Himself." (II Timothy 2:13) Without His grace, love and faithfulness I would not have a chance. "What if some did not have faith? Will their lack of faith nullify God's faithfulness? Not at all! Let God be true, and every man a liar. As it is written: So that you may be proved right when you speak and prevail when you judge." (Romans 3:3-4)

Our Heavenly Father has plans for our lives. We need to submit to His will and authority. He is the One and Only Almighty Father in heaven. He is Sovereign. If He can create the world, then He is very capable of taking whatever mess that you have going on in your life and make a message out of it. "For I know the plans I have for you, declares the Lord, plans to prosper you and not to harm you, plans to give you hope and a future. Then you will call upon Me and come and pray to Me, and I will listen to you. You will seek Me and find Me when you seek Me with all your heart. I will be found by you, declares the Lord, and bring you back from captivity." (Jeremiah 29:11-14) Once you have accepted Jesus Christ into your heart, you are then a child of God. He will always be faithful to you. You will go through many trials, but He will always be there for you. He will help you through them and provide a way out. "So, if you think you are standing firm, be careful that you don't fall! No temptation has seized you except what is common to man. And God is faithful; He will not let you be tempted beyond what you can bear. But when you are tempted, He will also provide a way out so that you can stand up under it." (I Corinthians 10:12-13)

Pray and ask the Holy Spirit to bring to your remembrance the many times God has shown Himself faithful to you. Record them below as a memory you can look back on for encouragement.

Sandra Lott

29. El Hakabodh: The God of Glory

(Psalm 29:3) "The voice of the Lord is over the waters; the God of glory thunders, the Lord thunders over the mighty waters."

You must think about the things in life that you are giving your devotion to; are you giving your devotion to the lusts of the world; which will pass away and take your soul with it? "Do not love the world or anything in the world. If anyone loves the world, the love of the Father is not in him. For everything in the world-- the cravings of sinful man, the lust of his eyes and the boasting of what he has and does-- comes not from the Father but from the world. The world and its desires pass away, but the man who does the will of God lives forever." (I John 2:15-17) Or, are you giving your devotion and worship to God who is eternal?

Where Has All the Worship Gone?

Where is the worship? Where has is gone?

The world promotes drinking and drugs and the latest Harry Potter Book in the now. It promotes witchcraft in which You are against. You parted the Red Sea and healed the blind and the sick. Where is Your praise? Where has it gone?

People talk about who did what to whom and that seems to be ok, but talk about my Savior, the One who died for me, and something's wrong with me. I'm just another fanatic. Why is that so? Where is Your worship?

A crown of thorns dug into Your head and nails pierced Your feet. You took our pain and our punishment. You died for us. Where has Your worship gone?

People sit around on Sunday's and watch the latest football game, but go to the house of God; they don't have time for that. You gave Your life, but that is not important enough. Where has all Your worship gone?

Blood ran down Your face, nails pierced your feet. You died for us.

Where has all Your worship gone?

The world does us wrong in some way every day. Do we leave it? Someone in church, human that they are, does us wrong and we leave it. The house of God! Your house where we go to worship, You and not the people who go there! Where has Your worship gone?

You carried the cross and was beaten and whipped beyond human recognition.

Where has Your worship gone?

There's violence, killing and stealing overflowing in the world and watching desperate housewives seems to be the latest craze. Where is Your worship?

You shed tears for us. You sweat drops of blood before hanging on the cross. You were beaten, laughed at and spit on. A whip marred Your back. Your body was covered in blood. You hung on the cross. You took our pain. You died for us. Where is the gratitude for what You did? Where has all the worship gone? Where is the glory, honor and praise due Your holy name?

What importance have you given to God? Do you worship Him as the God Most High or are there many idols in your life? We are only to have one God and that is God Almighty, everything else is an idol. An idol is, according to Webster's New American Dictionary, an image of a God, used as an object of worship or an object of ardent or excessive devotion. According to the words of this dictionary an idol is something that you worship and anything that you worship is your lord or master. "For a man is a slave to whatever has mastered him." (II Peter 2:19) There should be only one who is master over you and that is the Lord your God. "You shall have no other gods before me." (Exodus 20:3) What kind of idols do you have in your life? What kind of addictions have mastered you? Are you truly worshipping the Lord your God as you should? "You ought to live holy and godly lives as you look forward to the day of God and speed its coming." (II Peter 3:11-12) Just as the Israelites were delayed entering the Promised Land due to their disobedience, your victory may be delayed for the same reason, although that is not always the case. Examine your heart and soul, and see how much of the delay that you may be experiencing is your own fault or things yet for you to learn before you can move on. God will not allow you to move forward if you are not ready to handle what is ahead. It may cause you to fall if you move prematurely, and take away from the glory that He would receive. When He is glorified not only your life is changed, but those around you will change as well.

Ask the Holy Spirit to speak to your heart. How does He want to glorify His Holy Name through you?

_____

_____

_____

_____

_____

_____

_____

_____

_____

∿∿∿∿∿∿

Facebook Connect: Post one of the names of God on the FB page each day as you read and comment on how God has been that to you.

Chapter 3
The Cross: Salvation

Up to this point we have talked about who He is and about His love for all of mankind. You need to know that! You need to know about His unconditional love, and the many different facets of who He is to you before you can truly comprehend the overwhelming act of love He did on the cross. So, if up to this point you are not saved, maybe learning about His love and who He is will help you to cross that line and receive Him as Lord and Savior. If the previous chapters were not enough, then that is what this chapter is all about. You cannot go any deeper in a relationship with Him until you first become His, His child.

Sin was so rampant and due to intermarrying, not nationalities, but differing faiths is what led the Israelites astray. God says to come out from them and be separate, that is to protect you and to keep you from wandering away from Him. It is for your benefit that you stay close to Him and do not waiver in your faith, and not to have a "holier than thou attitude." "Therefore, "Come out from them and be separate, says the Lord. Touch no unclean thing, and I will receive you." (II Corinthians 6:17) But you may ask, I have done too much, how can I? I am not worthy. But that is the beauty of what Jesus Christ did on the cross for us. He is the Son of God, completely without sin and He was made sin for us so by our faith in Him, and acceptance of what He did, He becomes our atonement! "The Lord looked and was displeased that there was no justice. He saw that there was no one, he was appalled that there was no one to intervene; so His own arm achieved salvation for Him, and His own righteousness sustained Him. He put on righteousness as His breastplate, and the helmet of salvation on His head; He put on the garments of vengeance and wrapped Himself in zeal as in a cloak." (Isaiah 59:15-17)

Jesus Christ, Son of God, came down from heaven to take the punishment for our sins, so He could have us with Him in eternity. "For God so loved the world that he gave his one and only Son, that whoever believes in him shall not perish but have eternal life." (John 3:16) You may ask why, why is that necessary? Let me answer that by asking a question. You see all the hate in the world, the stealing, the bullying, the killing, abuse, drug addiction and the pain and heartache it causes, the infidelity. That is darkness and evil, and eternity is forever. Do you want that same evil in eternity? So, with that in mind, if you do not receive Him, it is your choice, but it will also be your choice where you spend eternity. "For the wages of sin is death, but the gift of God is eternal life in Christ Jesus our Lord." (Romans 6:23) I for one do not, and that is why we need Jesus, by His death and resurrection and upon receiving Him as Lord, asking Him into your heart, you are filled with His Holy Spirit and your heart is changed and you are made new. "Therefore, if anyone is in Christ, the new creation has come: The old has gone, the new is here!" (II Corinthians 5:17) His love fills you completely. He became our righteousness and our peace, and upon our acceptance, we have access to that.

"Who has believed our message and to whom has the arm of the Lord been revealed? He grew up before Him like a tender shoot, and like a root out of dry ground. He had no beauty or majesty to attract us to Him, nothing in His appearance that we should desire Him. He was despised and rejected by mankind, a man of suffering, and familiar with pain. Like one from whom people hide their faces He was despised, and we held Him in low esteem. Surely, He took up our pain and bore our suffering, yet we considered him punished by God, stricken by Him, and afflicted. But He was pierced for our transgressions, He was crushed for our iniquities; the punishment that brought us peace was on Him, and by His wounds, we are healed. We all, like sheep, have gone astray, each of us has turned to our own way, and the Lord has laid on Him the iniquity of us all. He was oppressed and afflicted, yet He did not open His mouth; He was led like a lamb to the slaughter, and as a sheep before its shearers is silent, so He did not open His mouth. By oppression and judgment, He was taken away. Yet who of His generation protested? For He was cut off from the land of the living; for the transgression of my people, He was punished. He was assigned a grave with the wicked, and with the rich in His death, though He had done no violence, nor was any deceit in His mouth. Yet it was the Lord's will to crush Him and cause Him to suffer, and though the Lord makes His life an offering for sin, He will see His offspring and prolong his days, and the will of the Lord will prosper in His hand. After He has suffered, He will see the

light of life and be satisfied; by His knowledge, my righteous servant will justify many, and He will bear their iniquities. Therefore, I will give Him a portion among the great, and He will divide the spoils with the strong, because He poured out His life unto death, and was numbered with the transgressors. For He bore the sin of many, and made intercession for the transgressors." (Isaiah 53)

He was without sin and became sin for us and paid the price for our sins and you do not have to do anything, you just have to come. "Therefore, since we have such a great high priest who has passed through the heavens, Jesus the Son of God, let us hold firmly to what we profess. For we do not have a high priest who is unable to empathize with our weaknesses, but we have one who has been tempted in every way, just as we are--yet He did not sin." (Hebrews 4:14-15) That is what His grace is all about, a gift. "As for you, you were dead in your transgressions and sins, in which you used to live when you followed the ways of this world, and of the ruler of the kingdom of the air, the spirit who is now at work in those who are disobedient. All of us also lived among them at one time, gratifying the cravings of our flesh and following its desires and thoughts. Like the rest, we were by nature deserving of wrath. But because of his great love for us, God, who is rich in mercy, made us alive with Christ even when we were dead in transgressions—it is by grace you have been saved. And God raised us up with Christ and seated us with him in the heavenly realms in Christ Jesus, in order that in the coming ages he might show the incomparable

riches of his grace, expressed in his kindness to us in Christ
Jesus. For it is by grace you have been saved, through
faith—and this is not from yourselves, it is the gift of
God—not by works, so that no one can boast." (Ephesians
2:1-9)

There is no possible way that you have done too much
that the blood of Jesus will not cover. "This is the message
we have heard from him and declare to you: God is light;
in Him, there is no darkness at all. If we claim to have
fellowship with Him and yet walk in the darkness, we lie
and do not live out the truth. But if we walk in the light, as
He is in the light, we have fellowship with one another, and
the blood of Jesus, His Son, purifies us from all sin. If we
claim to be without sin, we deceive ourselves and the truth
is not in us. If we confess our sins, He is faithful and just
and will forgive us our sins and purify us from all
unrighteousness." (I John 1:5-9) No one is without sin, you
are not isolated. In the light of a holy God, we are made of
flesh and the flesh is weak, we have all sinned. "For all
have sinned and fall short of the glory of God." (Romans
3:23)

Jesus was beaten beyond any resemblance of human
recognition, His hands and feet nailed to a cross, a crown
of thorns placed on His head with blood running down
His face, and He was without sin and He did that for
us. "See, my servant will act wisely; He will be raised and
lifted up and highly exalted. Just as there were many who
were appalled at Him—His appearance was so disfigured
beyond that of any human being and His form marred
beyond human likeness—so He will sprinkle many nations,
and kings will shut their mouths because of Him. For what

they were not told, they will see, and what they have not heard, they will understand." (Isaiah 52:13-15) So, there is no sin too big that the blood of the sinless Son of God will not cover!

Jesus Christ took your punishment, all you have to do is believe and receive.

"But what does it say? "The word is near you; it is in your mouth and in your heart," that is, the message concerning faith that we proclaim: If you declare with your mouth, "Jesus is Lord," and believe in your heart that God raised him from the dead, you will be saved. For it is with your heart that you believe and are justified, and it is with your mouth that you profess your faith and are saved. As Scripture says, "Anyone who believes in him will never be put to shame." For there is no difference between Jew and Gentile—the same Lord is Lord of all and richly blesses all who call on him, for, "Everyone who calls on the name of the Lord will be saved." (Romans 10:8-13)

Acts 9:1-22: Paul's Conversion

"Meanwhile, Saul was still breathing out murderous threats against the Lord's disciples. He went to the high priest and asked him for letters to the synagogues in Damascus, so that if he found any there who belonged to the Way, whether men or women, he might take them as prisoners to Jerusalem. As he neared Damascus on his journey, suddenly a light from heaven flashed around him.

He fell to the ground and heard a voice say to him, "Saul, Saul, why do you persecute Me?" "Who are you, Lord?" Saul asked. "I am Jesus, whom you are persecuting," he replied. "Now get up and go into the city, and you will be told what you must do." The men traveling with Saul stood there speechless; they heard the sound but did not see anyone. Saul got up from the ground, but when he opened his eyes he could see nothing.

So, they led him by the hand into Damascus. For three days he was blind, and did not eat or drink anything. In Damascus, there was a disciple named Ananias. The Lord called to him in a vision, "Ananias!" "Yes, Lord," he answered. The Lord told him, "Go to the house of Judas on Straight Street and ask for a man from Tarsus named Saul, for he is praying. In a vision, he has seen a man named Ananias come and place his hands on him to restore his sight." "Lord," Ananias answered, "I have heard many reports about this man and all the harm he has done to your holy people in Jerusalem. And he has come here with authority from the chief priests to arrest all who call on Your name." But the Lord said to Ananias, "Go! This man is My chosen instrument to proclaim My name to the Gentiles and their kings and to the people of Israel. I will show him how much he must suffer for My name."

Then Ananias went to the house and entered it. Placing his hands on Saul, he said, "Brother Saul, the Lord—Jesus, who appeared to you on the road as you were coming here—has sent me so that you may see again and be filled with the Holy Spirit." Immediately, something like scales fell from Saul's eyes, and he could see again. He got up and was baptized, and after taking some food, he regained his strength.

Saul spent several days with the disciples in Damascus. At once he began to preach in the synagogues that Jesus is the Son of God. All those who heard him were astonished and asked, "Isn't he the man who raised havoc in Jerusalem among those who call on this Name? And hasn't he come here to take them as prisoners to the chief priests?" Yet Saul grew more and more powerful and baffled the Jews living in Damascus by proving that Jesus is the Messiah."

In the passage above, what was it that Paul, who was known as Saul before, doing? He was having Christians, those who believed in Jesus and were preaching His name, killed. That is murder. How can your sin be any worse? The Lord blinded him, symbolically blinding him to the evil that was leading him astray and by the use of Ananias as His vessel, He opened His eyes to the truth. Paul was led to Straight street, also symbolically speaking that Jesus is the only way, the only STRAIGHT way to Jesus. "A voice of one calling in the wilderness, 'Prepare the way for the Lord, make straight paths for Him." (Mark 1:3) Jesus is the only way to eternal life. "Jesus answered, "I am the way and the truth and the life. No one comes to the Father except through Me." (John 14:6)

Record your heart to the Lord for His unconditional love for us on the lines below. Then if you have not received Him as Lord, pray the prayer at the end. Welcome to the family of God. Then find a good church to go to. This will help you to be spiritually fed, if you do not know of one, ask! The Holy Spirit will lead you, then let the Pastor know that you just received Jesus as Lord and ask him what to do next.

_____

_____

_____

_____

_____

_____

_____

_____

_____

_____

_____

_____

_____

_____

_____

_____

_____

_____

_____

_____

_____

_____

_____

_____

_____

_____

_____

_____

_____

_____

_____

_____

Prayer of Salvation

Dear Almighty Father in heaven, I know that I am a sinner and I ask your forgiveness of all my sins. I want to make You the Lord of my life and I want to serve You all the days of my life. I believe that Jesus Christ died on the cross for my sins. Thank you so much for loving me and waiting on me to come to the knowledge of the truth! Thank you for my salvation. Please help me and guide me in learning your Word so I can be a light to the world. Please, Jesus, come into my heart, and baptize me with Your Holy Spirit. I thank You, and praise Your Holy Name, and ask all this in the Name of Jesus Christ our Lord. Amen.

_____

_____

_____

_____

_____

_____

_____

_____

_____

_____

_____

_____

_____

_____

_____

_____

_____

_____

_____

_____

_____

_____

_____

_____

_____

∿∿∿∿∿

Facebook Connect: Post to the FB page what the cross means to and share your testimony!

Chapter 4
Prayer Life

Developing a prayer life in another important part of drawing closer to God and having a deeper relationship with Him. Your prayer life should not be just about your "911" list of I want or needs, but it is also communication. Communication involves talking and listening. Talk to God, in respect, but as a friend. "One who has unreliable friends soon comes to ruin, but there is a friend who sticks closer than a brother." (Proverbs 18:24) Set a time that you spend with God every day. You would do that for a friend, your husband or wife, girlfriend or boyfriend, wouldn't you? So, why not for God? But also, talk to Him all through the day in your spirit.

God knows your heart and that is what He wants. "A person may think their own ways are right, but the Lord weighs the heart." (Proverbs 21:2) God wants sincerity not what you may think what will look good to Him, He does not want show, He wants you. "But the Lord said to Samuel, "Do not consider his appearance or his height, for

I have rejected him. The Lord does not look at the things people look at. People look at the outward appearance, but the Lord looks at the heart." (I Samuel 16:7) Just be yourself, He already knows your heart and what is on it anyway. So, just be you and it will help you to break free from thinking you have to put on a show or use fancy words, you cannot sugarcoat anything with God. This will help you tear down any walls you have erected from wrong preconceived ideas of how you think you need to approach Him. "O Lord, you have searched me and you know me. You know when I sit and when I rise; you perceive my thoughts from afar. You discern my going out and my lying down; you are familiar with all my ways. Before a word is on my tongue you know it completely, O Lord." (Psalm 139:1-4)

1. In Luke 18: 9-14 there were two men who came to the temple to pray. Read the passage below, and then answer the question.

"To some who were confident of their own righteousness and looked down on everyone else, Jesus told this parable: "Two men went up to the temple to pray, one a Pharisee and the other a tax collector. The Pharisee stood by himself and prayed: 'God, I thank you that I am not like other people—robbers, evildoers, adulterers—or even like this tax collector. I fast twice a week and give a tenth of all I get.' "But the tax collector stood at a distance. He would not even look up to heaven, but beat his breast and said,

'God, have mercy on me, a sinner.' "I tell you that this man, rather than the other, went home justified before God. For all those who exalt themselves will be humbled, and those who humble themselves will be exalted."

A. Which man prayed with a sincere heart and which man prayed for show, approval by men and not God?

_____

_____

_____

B. If you are praying to God, to draw closer to Him, then why do you need to care about what others think?

_____

_____

_____

2. In this passage Luke 18:15-30 what is Jesus trying to covey about coming to Him? Now, look into your own heart and ask the Holy Spirit to reveal to you areas you need to grow in this matter. Record on the lines below, noting this is for your remembrance and to help you draw closer to God.

The Little Children and Jesus

"People were also bringing babies to Jesus for him to place his hands on them. When the disciples saw this, they rebuked them. But Jesus called the children to him and said, "Let the little children come to me, and do not hinder them, for the kingdom of God belongs to such as these. Truly I tell you, anyone who will not receive the kingdom of God like a little child will never enter it.""

The Rich and the Kingdom of God

A certain ruler asked him, "Good teacher, what must I do to inherit eternal life?" "Why do you call me good?" Jesus answered. "No one is good—except God alone. You know the commandments: 'You shall not commit adultery, you shall not murder, you shall not steal, you shall not give false testimony, honor your father and mother." "All these I have kept since I was a boy," he said. When Jesus heard this, he said to him, "You still lack one thing. Sell everything you have and give to the poor, and you will have treasure in heaven. Then come, follow me." When he heard this, he became very sad, because he was very wealthy. Jesus looked at him and said, "How hard it is for the rich to enter the kingdom of God! Indeed, it is easier for a camel to go through the eye of a needle than for someone who is rich to enter the kingdom of God." Those who heard this asked, "Who then can be saved?" Jesus replied, "What is impossible with man is possible with God." Peter said to him, "We have left all we had to follow you!" "Truly I tell you," Jesus said to them, "no one who has left home or wife or brothers or sisters or parents or children for the sake of the kingdom of God will fail to receive many times as much in this age, and in the age to come eternal life."

_____

_____

_____

_____

_____

_____

_____

_____

_____

_____

_____

_____

_____

3. Besides being sincere, another part of your prayer life is being persistent, having faith and not giving up. If your faith is lacking, ask, He says ask and you shall receive. "Until now you have not asked for anything in my name. Ask and you will receive, and your joy will be complete." (John 16:24) Then keep asking, do not give up. If you do not have faith, then why are you asking?

Luke 18:1-8--The Parable of the Persistent Widow

Then Jesus told his disciples a parable to show them that they should always pray and not give up. He said: "In a certain town there was a judge who neither feared God nor cared what people thought. And there was a widow in that town who kept coming to him with the plea, 'Grant me justice against my adversary.' "For some time, he refused. But finally he said to himself, 'Even though I don't fear God or care what people think, yet because this widow keeps bothering me, I will see that she gets justice, so that she won't eventually come and attack me!" And the Lord said, "Listen to what the unjust judge says. And will not God bring about justice for his chosen ones, who cry out to him day and night? Will he keep putting them off? I tell you, he will see that they get justice, and quickly. However, when the Son of Man comes, will he find faith on the earth?"

Have you been persistent in your prayers? Do you give God the time and trust deserved to answer your prayers in His time and in His way, His perfect way? Ask the Holy Spirit to reveal to you areas that you need your faith increased. Ask for His help.

_____

_____

_____

_____

_____

_____

_____

_____

_____

_____

_____

_____

_____

Developing an intimate prayer life, one that is from a sincere heart in full devotion to God is imperative in creating a deeper more intimate relationship with Him.

"Let us draw near to God with a sincere heart and with the full assurance that faith brings, having our hearts sprinkled to cleanse us from a guilty conscience and having our bodies washed with pure water." (Hebrews 10:22) Record any other thoughts, revelations or prayers below.

_____

_____

_____

_____

_____

_____

_____

_____

_____

_____

Sandra Lott

∿∿∿∿∿∿

Facebook Connect: Post to the FB a heartfelt prayer to God, or ways this devotion has helped you to add meaning to your prayer life.

Chapter 5
Admit-I Did What? Sin & Forgiveness

Refusing to admit when you are wrong about something, when you have sinned is another big roadblock. It will keep you from becoming more intimate with Jesus. It is like seeing weeds in a garden that are overtaking it, and calling them plants. The weeds will continue to grow and overtake it until there is no room left for the real flowers or other plants that are in the garden. This is just like the fruit of the Spirit planted in our hearts as seeds upon our conversion. The fruit needs nurtured, watered by time spent with God, obeying Him and reading His Word. But, if you leave a lot of negative emotions, sins and refusing to forgive, these negative emotions and sins will overtake your heart and keep you from growing. It will keep the fruit from blossoming within your heart.

Allowing the Holy Spirit to convict you, teach you what you are doing wrong, and correct you helps you to grow.

"Therefore, since we are surrounded by such a great cloud of witnesses, let us throw off everything that hinders and the sin that so easily entangles. And let us run with perseverance the race marked out for us, fixing our eyes on Jesus, the pioneer and perfecter of faith. For the joy set before him he endured the cross, scorning its shame, and sat down at the right hand of the throne of God. Consider Him who endured such opposition from sinners, so that you will not grow weary and lose heart. In your struggle against sin, you have not yet resisted to the point of shedding your blood. And have you completely forgotten this word of encouragement that addresses you as a father addresses his son? It says, "My son, do not make light of the Lord's discipline, and do not lose heart when He rebukes you, because the Lord disciplines the one He loves, and He chastens everyone He accepts as His son.""

Endure hardship as discipline; God is treating you as His children. For what children are not disciplined by their father? If you are not disciplined—and everyone undergoes discipline—then you are not legitimate, not true sons and daughters at all. Moreover, we have all had human fathers who disciplined us, and we respected them for it. How much more should we submit to the Father of spirits and live! They disciplined us for a little while as they thought best; but God disciplines us for our good, in order that we may share in His holiness. No discipline seems pleasant at the time, but painful. Later on, however, it produces a harvest of righteousness and peace for those who have been trained by it. Therefore, strengthen your feeble arms and weak knees. "Make level paths for your feet," so that the lame may not be disabled, but rather healed." (Hebrews

12:1-13)   Otherwise, if you refuse to allow the Holy Spirit to work in you, putting on pride and stubbornness, it will hinder you. "Pride goes before destruction, a haughty spirit before a fall." (Proverbs 16:18)

As you learn and grow your mind is renewed and transformed. "Therefore, I urge you, brothers and sisters, in view of God's mercy, to offer your bodies as a living sacrifice, holy and pleasing to God—this is your true and proper worship. Do not conform to the pattern of this world, but be transformed by the renewing of your mind. Then you will be able to test and approve what God's will is—his good, pleasing and perfect will." (Romans 12:1-2) You learn the truth and the truth is what frees you from what kept you bound and not growing before. "Then you will know the truth, and the truth will set you free." (John 8:32)

After you have learned from your sins and wrong beliefs, you can in turn help other. They can learn from your example, your testimony as said in Hebrews 12:12-13, "Therefore, strengthen your feeble arms and weak knees. "Make level paths for your feet," so that the lame may not be disabled, but rather healed."

Admitting your sins as well as learning to forgive, allows the Holy Spirit room in your heart to correct and teach you. This keeps you growing and drawing closer and closer to God, going from glory to glory. "But we all, with open face beholding as in a glass the glory of the Lord, are changed into the same image from glory to glory, even as by the Spirit of the Lord." (Ii Corinthians 3:18)

If you still refuse to allow the Holy Spirit to correct you, you refuse to forgive others, the roadblock will stay in your path and will lead to further discipline and trials. "But he gives us more grace. That is why Scripture says: "God opposes the proud but shows favor to the humble." (James 4:6) It is in humility that you grow and find God's favor. "Likewise, you younger, submit yourselves unto the elder. Yea, all of you be subject one to another, and be clothed with humility: for God resists the proud, and gives grace to the humble." (I Peter 5:5)

Jacob's name means, "Deceiver." What did he do in Genesis 25:19-24 and again in Genesis 27. Read these chapters and on through chapter 28. Did Jacob ever admit, own up to what he did?

_____

_____

_____

_____

_____

_____

_____

_____

_____

Jacob prayed at Bethel on his way to his uncle's after he had a dream from God. He prayed for God to watch over him, but he never admitted what he did. As parents, even when our children do wrong, we are not happy with them when they do but they are still our children and we are still going to love them and take care of them. If you continue to read even further, you will see he was deceived by his uncle Laban. You do reap what you sow. "Do not be deceived: God cannot be mocked. A man reaps what he sows. Whoever sows to please their flesh, from the flesh will reap destruction; whoever sows to please the Spirit, from the Spirit will reap eternal life." (Galatians 6:7-8)

Laban deceived him into working for him seven years to marry Rachel. When Jacob completed the seven years Laban gave him his other daughter, Leah instead. How can you not know? Anyway, he had to work for Laban another seven years in order to marry Rachel. Your sin, although a child of God, will keep you longer than you want to stay in the trial it produces and from moving on in the path you desire.

Finally, upon leaving to return home, at the thought of seeing his brother Esau, Jacob had to come to terms with himself and admit. On the way he prayed to God, he was afraid. He remembered his brother's anger. He was admitting to himself, finally, through praying his deception of years ago.

Genesis 32:1-30

"Jacob also went on his way, and the angels of God met him. When Jacob saw them, he said, "This is the camp of God!" So, he named that place Mahanaim. Jacob sent messengers ahead of him to his brother Esau in the land of Seir, the country of Edom. He instructed them: "This is what you are to say to my lord Esau: 'Your servant Jacob says, I have been staying with Laban and have remained there till now. I have cattle and donkeys, sheep and goats, male and female servants. Now I am sending this message to my lord, that I may find favor in your eyes.'" When the messengers returned to Jacob, they said, "We went to your brother Esau, and now he is coming to meet you, and four hundred men are with him." In great fear and distress Jacob divided the people who were with him into two groups, and the flocks and herds and camels as well. He thought, "If Esau comes and attacks one group, the group that is left may escape."

Then Jacob prayed, "O God of my father Abraham, God of my father Isaac, LORD, you who said to me, 'Go back to your country and your relatives, and I will make you prosper,' I am unworthy of all the kindness and faithfulness you have shown your servant. I had only my staff when I crossed this Jordan, but now I have become two camps. Save me, I pray, from the hand of my brother Esau, for I am afraid he will come and attack me, and also the mothers with their children. But you have said, 'I will surely make you prosper and will make your descendants like the sand of the sea, which cannot be counted.'" He spent the night there, and from what he had with him he selected a gift for his brother Esau: wo hundred female goats and twenty male goats, two hundred ewes and twenty rams, thirty female camels with their young, forty cows and ten bulls, and twenty female donkeys and ten male donkeys. He put them in the care of his servants, each herd by itself, and said to his servants, "Go ahead of me, and keep some space between the herds."

He instructed the one in the lead: "When my brother Esau meets you and asks, 'Who do you belong to, and where are you going, and who owns all these animals in front of you?' then you are to say, 'They belong to your servant Jacob. They are a gift sent to my lord Esau, and he is coming behind us.'" He also instructed the second, the third and all the others who followed the herds: "You are to say the same thing to Esau when you meet him.   "And be sure to say, 'Your servant Jacob is coming behind us.' " For he thought, "I will pacify him with these gifts I am sending on ahead; later, when I see him, perhaps he will receive me." So, Jacob's gifts went on ahead of him, but he himself spent the night in the camp.

Jacob Wrestles With God

That night Jacob got up and took his two wives, his two female servants and his eleven sons and crossed the ford of the Jabbok. After he had sent them across the stream, he sent over all his possessions. So, Jacob was left alone, and a man wrestled with him till daybreak. When the man saw that he could not overpower him, he touched the socket of Jacob's hip so that his hip was wrenched as he wrestled with the man. Then the man said, "Let me go, for it is daybreak." But Jacob replied, "I will not let you go unless you bless me." The man asked him, "What is your name?"

"Jacob," he answered. Then the man said, "Your name will no longer be Jacob, but Israel, because you have struggled with God and with humans and have overcome." Jacob said, "Please tell me your name." But he replied, "Why do you ask my name?" Then he blessed him there. So, Jacob called the place Peniel, saying, "It is because I saw God face to face, and yet my life was spared."

The night before meeting Esau he sends gifts ahead of him in order to sooth his brother's anger. God wanted complete surrender, admission as well. "Therefore, if you are offering your gift at the altar and there remember that your brother or sister has something against you, leave your gift there in front of the altar. First go and be reconciled to them; then come and offer your gift." (Matthew 5:23-24) It turns out through reading how Esau greeted Jacob, he had already forgiven him.

That night he also wrestles with an Angel of God. This was his inner struggle. Have you had to come to terms with something you have done? Or maybe someone you have not forgiven, and it has created a heaviness in your heart from the anger you have held onto? It will continue to hinder you until you make amends and repent of your sin. Admit, repent and move on! "Praise the Lord, my soul; all my inmost being, praise His holy name. Praise the Lord, my soul, and forget not all His benefits—who forgives all your sins and heals all your diseases, who redeems your life from the pit and crowns you with love and compassion, who satisfies your desires with good things so that your youth is renewed like the eagle's." (Psalm 103:1-5)

Besides admitting your sins, you cannot move on until you forgive. How can you expect God Almighty to forgive your sins, sins that He died on the cross in your place to forgive, and you not forgive those who wrong you? You are placing yourself above Him in doing that. "For if you forgive other people when they sin against you, your heavenly Father will also forgive you. "But if you do not forgive others their sins, your Father will not forgive your sins." (Matthew 6:14-15)

Ask the Holy Spirit to reveal all those people you may still need to forgive. He will also give you the strength in which to do it, and in return you will receive His healing love that will bring peace to your spirit. "I can do all things through Christ who gives me strength." (Philippians 4:13) The best thing about God forgiving you, is one He has forgiven you, He forgets it! Wow! Isn't that wonderful! "For I will forgive their wickedness and will remember their sins no more." (Hebrews 8:12) Ask Him to reveal any sins you still need to repent for and record your thoughts and prayers below.

_____

_____

_____

_____

_____

_____

_____

_____

_____

_____

_____

_____

_____

_____

_____

_____

Sandra Lott

Facebook Connect: Post to the FB how this devotion helped you to search yourself and also make amends.

Chapter 6

Surrender! Oh No!

ℒearning to surrender, to give up our will when our flesh is screaming no! "You, my brothers and sisters, were called to be free. But do not use your freedom to indulge the flesh; rather, serve one another humbly in love. For the entire law is fulfilled in keeping this one command: "Love your neighbor as yourself." If you bite and devour each other, watch out or you will be destroyed by each other. So I say, walk by the Spirit, and you will not gratify the desires of the flesh. For the flesh desires what is contrary to the Spirit, and the Spirit what is contrary to the flesh. They are in conflict with each other, so that you are not to do whatever you want. But if you are led by the Spirit, you are not under the law." (Galatians 5:13-18) That is something very hard to do, but is another part of our spiritual growth process that will draw you ever closer to God.

Jesus Christ learned obedience and we, through His Holy Spirit can have this same will and mind and attitude of obedience. It is our love and devotion to God, when that grows it becomes more important to please Him, than to satisfy our own needs.

"Therefore if you have any encouragement from being united with Christ, if any comfort from His love, if any common sharing in the Spirit, if any tenderness and compassion, then make my joy complete by being like-minded, having the same love, being one in spirit and of one mind. Do nothing out of selfish ambition or vain conceit. Rather, in humility value others above yourselves, not looking to your own interests but each of you to the interests of the others. In your relationships with one another, have the same mindset as Christ Jesus: Who, being in very nature God, did not consider equality with God something to be used to His own advantage; rather, He made Himself nothing by taking the very nature of a servant, being made in human likeness. And being found in appearance as a man, He humbled Himself by becoming obedient to death—even death on a cross! Therefore, God exalted Him to the highest place and gave Him the name that is above every name, that at the name of Jesus every knee should bow, in heaven and on earth and under the earth, and every tongue acknowledge that Jesus Christ is Lord, to the glory of God the Father. Therefore, my dear friends, as you have always obeyed—not only in my presence, but now much more in my absence—continue to work out your salvation with fear and trembling, for it is God who works in you to will and to act in order to fulfill his good purpose. Do everything without grumbling or arguing so that you may become blameless and pure, children of God without fault in a warped and crooked

generation." Then you will shine among them like stars in the sky as you hold firmly to the word of life. And then I will be able to boast on the day of Christ that I did not run or labor in vain. But even if I am being poured out like a drink offering on the sacrifice and service coming from your faith, I am glad and rejoice with all of you. So, you too should be glad and rejoice with me." (*Philippians 2:1-18*)

With His Holy Spirit within us, we do have the strength to surrender our will and obey Him, putting Him first, rather than our own wants. As we do and pass through the difficult trials of life we grow and our life becomes a blessing and a testimony to those around us. We are then able to help and encourage others because we have been through difficulties, surrendered to His will and obeyed. "Praise be to the God and Father of our Lord Jesus Christ, the Father of compassion and the God of all comfort, who comforts us in all our troubles, so that we can comfort those in any trouble with the comfort we ourselves receive from God. For just as we share abundantly in the sufferings of Christ, so also our comfort abounds through Christ. If we are distressed, it is for your comfort and salvation; if we are comforted, it is for your comfort, which produces in you patient endurance of the same sufferings we suffer. And our hope for you is firm, because we know that just as you share in our sufferings, so also you share in our comfort." (II Corinthians 1:3-7)

Surrendering to God's will is humility and with it and obedience, comes God's favor; "Humility is the fear of the

Lord; its wages are riches and honor and life." (Proverbs 22:4)

I Died Today

Lifeless in Your hands, You carry me.

I am dead to the world and to my flesh
that You may live free in me.

I have fought and wrestled against the struggles
in my heart, wanting all the pain to be free from me.

The answers to my pain You already knew.
There was only one thing that I needed to do.

Yet I struggled on, trying in my own way and
praying in desperation. The fight continued on;
my heart truly broken. I cry out, "Please God,
show me Your way!"

You knew the way and were patient with my stubborn
heart; fighting for its own way and failing to see it Yours.

Weary from the pain and the trials that wore me out; I fall
lifeless into Your hands. The path has broken my heart.

I finally died today. My will inside me gone.
It's buried with my pain and in Your hands I lay.

My heart cries out, "I'm tired Lord, there's no
more fight, my heart struggles no more."

To my amazement, the peace I sought finally came.
When to my will I died, and I called to You and gave
myself.
My heart will never be the same.

That was the way all along. For God is great and His way
is best. We must die to self and seek His grace;
in us let His glory be revealed that we may see His face.

He'll wait patiently to hear us say, "Lord, not my will,
but Thy will be done." His peace will come and you
will never be the same. When in your heart His
presence known, you will shine; His glory known
in Jesus name.

   In the book of Esther, Haman, who was one of the
king's nobles, hated the Jews and he plotted to kill them.
Esther had become queen but her background was not
known to the king or any of the officials. The date was set

to attack the Jews and something needed to be done. Esther needed to go to the king and Mordecai, her uncle instructed her to do so. She was afraid because in that time, you had to be summoned before you could approach the king or it was punishable by death.

What was she going to do? She was afraid and her human emotions, her flesh, did not want to do this; read the passage below and record what her uncle said, and what she did.

Esther 4: Mordecai Persuades Esther to Help

"When Mordecai learned of all that had been done, he tore his clothes, put on sackcloth and ashes, and went out into the city, wailing loudly and bitterly. But he went only as far as the king's gate, because no one clothed in sackcloth was allowed to enter it. In every province to which the edict and order of the king came, there was great mourning among the Jews, with fasting, weeping and wailing. Many lay in sackcloth and ashes. When Esther's eunuchs and female attendants came and told her about Mordecai, she was in great distress. She sent clothes for him to put on instead of his sackcloth, but he would not accept them. Then Esther summoned Hathak, one of the king's eunuchs assigned to attend her, and ordered him to find out what was troubling Mordecai and why.

So Hathak went out to Mordecai in the open square of the city in front of the king's gate. Mordecai told him everything that had happened to him, including the exact amount of money Haman had promised to pay into the royal treasury for the destruction of the Jews. He also gave him a copy of the text of the edict for their annihilation, which had been published in Susa, to show to Esther and explain it to her, and he told him to instruct her to go into the king's presence to beg for mercy and plead with him for her people. Hathak went back and reported to Esther what Mordecai had said. Then she instructed him to say to Mordecai, "All the king's officials and the people of the royal provinces know that for any man or woman who approaches the king in the inner court without being summoned the king has but one law: that they be put to death unless the king extends the gold scepter to them and spares their lives. But thirty days have passed since I was called to go to the king."

When Esther's words were reported to Mordecai, he sent back this answer: "Do not think that because you are in the king's house you alone of all the Jews will escape. For if you remain silent at this time, relief and deliverance for the Jews will arise from another place, but you and your father's family will perish. And who knows but that you have come to your royal position for such a time as this?" Then Esther sent this reply to Mordecai: "Go, gather together all the Jews who are in Susa, and fast for me. Do not eat or drink for three days, night or day. I and my attendants will fast as you do. When this is done, I will go to the king, even though it is against the law. And if I perish, I perish." So Mordecai went away and carried out all of Esther's instructions."

_____

_____

_____

_____

_____

_____

_____

_____

_____

_____

_____

_____

_____

Read through the next few chapters, 5-7. What happened as a result of Esther's obedience, to put the needs of others, which is God's will, above her own? "Do nothing out of selfish ambition or vain conceit. Rather, in humility value others above yourselves." (Philippians 2:3)

Sandra Lott

_____

_____

_____

_____

_____

_____

_____

_____

_____

_____

    Ask the Holy Spirit to reveal to you, areas that He has been leading you to surrender your will to His. Record them below as well as your emotions and concerns. Take those concerns to Him and allow Him to help you with them.

_____

_____

_____

_____

_____

_____

_____

_____

_____

_____

_____

_____

_____

_____

_____

_____

_____

_____

_____

_____

_____

_____

∿∿∿∿∿

Facebook Connect: Post to the FB the issues you have had in the past surrendering. How has this devotion inspired you to seek God's help in surrendering?

Chapter 7
Rocky Road Ahead: Trials

Trials are another part of our spiritual growth process that we do not like. We like our microwaves, fast food, nice cars and ones that work great with no mechanical trouble, air conditioning and heating, internet, television, cable, updated appliances and of course, who can live without their smart phone? When something goes wrong with one of them we kick and scream. We want it fixed and want it now! So, when trials come your way, it is just the same, you want it over immediately. When that happens, with most people, temper tantrums happen and you invite yourself to a pity party. That will keep you in the trial longer than you want to stay; it makes it "all about you."

That is not the direction God wants you to go in. He gave up the comforts of heaven to come in the flesh so He could understand us in our weaknesses. "Since the children have flesh and blood, He too shared in their humanity so that by His death he might break the power of him who holds the power of death—that is, the devil—and free those who all their lives were held in slavery by their fear of death. For surely it is not angels He helps, but

Abraham's descendants. For this reason He had to be made like them, fully human in every way, in order that He might become a merciful and faithful high priest in service to God, and that He might make atonement for the sins of the people. Because He Himself suffered when He was tempted, He is able to help those who are being tempted." (Hebrews 2:14-18)

Trials are a blessing! You are probably shaking your head right now in disagreement, especially if you are going through a rather difficult one. Trials will become a blessing once you go through them. "Consider it pure joy, my brothers and sisters, whenever you face trials of many kinds, because you know that the testing of your faith produces perseverance. Let perseverance finish its work so that you may be mature and complete, not lacking anything. If any of you lacks wisdom, you should ask God, who gives generously to all without finding fault, and it will be given to you. But when you ask, you must believe and not doubt, because the one who doubts is like a wave of the sea, blown and tossed by the wind. That person should not expect to receive anything from the Lord. Such a person is double-minded and unstable in all they do. Believers in humble circumstances ought to take pride in their high position. But the rich should take pride in their humiliation—since they will pass away like a wild flower. For the sun rises with scorching heat and withers the plant; its blossom falls and its beauty is destroyed. In the same way, the rich will fade away even while they go about their business. Blessed is the one who perseveres under trial because, having stood the test, that person will receive the

crown of life that the Lord has promised to those who love
Him. When tempted, no one should say, "God is tempting
me." For God cannot be tempted by evil, nor does he
tempt anyone; but each person is tempted when they are
dragged away by their own evil desire and enticed. Then,
after desire has conceived, it gives birth to sin; and sin,
when it is full-grown, gives birth to death. Don't be
deceived, my dear brothers and sisters. Every good and
perfect gift is from above, coming down from the Father
of the heavenly lights, who does not change like shifting
shadows. He chose to give us birth through the word of
truth, that we might be a kind of firstfruits of all he
created." (James 1:2-18)

Look back at the ones you have already been through.
You learned something after you went through, didn't you.
Record some of those times below for remembrance and
encouragement.

_____

_____

_____

_____

_____

_____

_____

_____

_____

_____

_____

_____

_____

One way to get through them is to speak the Word of God; it is alive and active. "For the word of God is alive and active. Sharper than any double-edged sword, it penetrates even to dividing soul and spirit, joints and marrow; it judges the thoughts and attitudes of the heart." (Hebrews 4:12) If God can create the world with His words, then with the Holy Spirit within you, His same words; alive and powerful, can do the same for you. "The Spirit gives life; the flesh counts for nothing. The words I have spoken to you--they are full of the Spirit and life." (John 6:63)

When you speak the words out loud, they penetrate into your heart increasing your faith and endurance to persevere; they give you hope. "So then faith comes by hearing, and hearing by the word of God." (Romans 10:17) God spoke, to a world that was formless and it came into being. Some things were started as a seed and He says in His Word, "As long as the earth endures, seedtime and harvest, cold and heat, summer and winter, day and night will never cease." (Genesis 8:22) So, just as God called them into existence, you can as well but give God time to work with your words to manifest them. "(As it is written, I have made you a father of many nations,) before him whom he believed, even God, who gives life to the dead, and calls those things which are not as though they were." (Romans 4:17)

So, how do you do this? By asking God to open your eyes to what He is trying to teach you, or a sin He is trying to convict you of or maybe a passion He wants to birth in you as a result of this trial. Then you read His Word and write down His promises regarding your situation and speaking them over your life, your family, yourself, your job and so on. "The tongue has the power of life and death, and those who love it will eat its fruit." (Proverbs 18:21) Don't give the devil ammunition by speaking negative words, your fears and what angers you. He will take that and run with it and bring about attacks, more trials! The very thing you are trying to get out of, instead speak God's promises, you will receive the fruit of them if you speak them in faith, believing. "Truly I tell you," Jesus replied, "if you have faith and do not doubt, not only will you do what was done to the fig tree, but even if you say to this mountain, 'Be lifted up and thrown into the sea,' it will happen. If you believe, you will receive whatever you ask for in prayer." (Matthew 21:21-22)

Acts 16:16-34—Paul in Prison

"Once when we were going to the place of prayer, we were met by a female slave who had a spirit by which she predicted the future. She earned a great deal of money for her owners by fortune-telling. She followed Paul and the rest of us, shouting, "These men are servants of the Most High God, who are telling you the way to be saved." She kept this up for many days. Finally Paul became so annoyed that he turned around and said to the spirit, "In the name of Jesus Christ I command you to come out of her!" At that moment the spirit left her. When her owners realized that their hope of making money was gone, they seized Paul and Silas and dragged them into the marketplace to face the authorities. They brought them before the magistrates and said, "These men are Jews, and are throwing our city into an uproar by advocating customs unlawful for us Romans to accept or practice."

The crowd joined in the attack against Paul and Silas, and the magistrates ordered them to be stripped and beaten with rods. After they had been severely flogged, they were thrown into prison, and the jailer was commanded to guard them carefully. When he received these orders, he put them in the inner cell and fastened their feet in the stocks. About midnight Paul and Silas were praying and singing hymns to God, and the other prisoners were listening to them. Suddenly there was such a violent earthquake that the foundations of the prison were

Page 200

shaken. At once all the prison doors flew open, and everyone's chains came loose. The jailer woke up, and when he saw the prison doors open, he drew his sword and was about to kill himself because he thought the prisoners had escaped. But Paul shouted, "Don't harm yourself! We are all here!"

The jailer called for lights, rushed in and fell trembling before Paul and Silas. He then brought them out and asked, "Sirs, what must I do to be saved?" They replied, "Believe in the Lord Jesus, and you will be saved—you and your household." Then they spoke the word of the Lord to him and to all the others in his house. At that hour of the night the jailer took them and washed their wounds; then immediately he and all his household were baptized. The jailer brought them into his house and set a meal before them; he was filled with joy because he had come to believe in God—he and his whole household.

What was Paul doing to be put in prison? He was not doing anything wrong by God's standards, but to those who did not believe he was; and that is the way it is today more than ever. The world will call your belief wrong, and twist it to say that you hate. Even though, if we call our self a child of God we are to continue to do what pleases Him regardless of the consequences. "Am I now trying to win the approval of human beings, or of God? Or am I trying to please people? If I were still trying to please people, I would not be a servant of Christ." (Galatians 1:10)

Sometimes you will go through trials just to open eyes of others and not because you did anything wrong. Thank

God that He chose to use you! "However, if you suffer as a Christian, do not be ashamed, but praise God that you bear that name." (I Peter 4:16)

With that said, what happened as a result of Paul's trial, his stay in prison? What was his attitude while in prison? His attitude helped his short stay in jail. How does that knowledge speak to you?

_____

_____

_____

_____

_____

_____

_____

_____

_____

_____

_____

_____

_____

_____

Ask the Holy Spirit to speak to your heart regarding a past trial or one that you are going through now. Ask Him to give you some wisdom, scriptures of hope and encouragement and a fresh revelation.

_____

_____

_____

_____

_____

_____

_____

_____

_____

_____

_____

_____

_____

_____

_____

_____

_____

_____

_____

_____

_____

_____

_____

_____

_____

_____

_____

_____

Sandra Lott

Facebook Connect: Post to the FB any new revelations you have learned through this devotion about going through trials and how to stay hopeful during them.

Step by Step Into a Deeper Walk in Christ

Chapter 8

Conquered Trails: Growth

Once you have been through a few trials and finally learned the peace that came in trusting God it has been engrained into you. Jesus is the one you run to for help and to keep you safe. "The name of the Lord is a strong tower: the righteous runs into it, and is safe." (Proverbs 18:10)

As you continue in the trials learning to call on the name of Jesus, your faith grows and you begin to trust Him, and know that He will be there for you. . "God is our refuge and strength, an ever-present help in trouble." (Psalm 46:1) This trust draws you closer and closer to Him. "Praise be to the God and Father of our Lord Jesus Christ! In His great mercy He has given us new birth into a living hope through the resurrection of Jesus Christ from the dead, and into an inheritance that can never perish, spoil or fade. This inheritance is kept in heaven for you, who through faith are shielded by God's power until the coming of the salvation that is ready to be revealed in the last time. In all this you greatly rejoice, though now for a little while you may have had to suffer grief in all kinds of trials. These have come so that the proven genuineness of your faith—of greater worth than gold, which perishes even though refined by fire—may result in praise, glory and honor when Jesus Christ is revealed. Though you have not seen Him, you love Him; and even though you do not see Him now, you believe in Him and are filled with an inexpressible and glorious joy, for you are receiving the end result of your faith, the salvation of your souls." (I Peter 1:3-9)

In some trials there will be periods of confessing His Word, and pressing in and through them in prayer and fasting. You will learn the importance of the Word of God and how speaking it gives you strength and peace within your heart. Praying His Word is one of the best ways to pray over someone or a situation because it is not tainted by human emotions or selfish desires. "I will worship toward Your holy temple, and praise Your name for your loving-kindness and for Your truth: for You have magnified Your Word above all Your name." (Psalm 138:2)

As you read the Word, confess it you will learn to hear His voice more clearly and know it is Him, and He will remind you of His Word right in the moment you need it. "But the Advocate, the Holy Spirit, whom the Father will send in My name, will teach you all things and will remind you of everything I have said to you." (John 14:26) This gives you hope and joy and strength to persevere because you know He is with you and will not fail you. "And the Lord, He it is that does go before you; He will be with you,

He will not fail you, neither forsake you: fear not, neither be dismayed." (Deuteronomy 31:8) You will not freak out so to speak, every time an onslaught of trials hit you. This is a sign that you have grown and matured in your Christian walk.

Then there will be times you need to just be still and wait on Him, "He says, "Be still, and know that I am God; I will be exalted among the nations, I will be exalted in the earth." (Psalm 46:10). There are times when God Almighty, El Shaddai, wants to step in and fight the battle for you and you just need to be still. I kind of like those times! "But Moses told the people, "Do not be afraid. Stand firm and you will see the Lord's salvation, which He will accomplish for you today; for the Egyptians you see today, you will never see again. The Lord will fight for you; you need only to be still." (Exodus 14:13-14)

In the story of Joseph, he was young, younger than all of his brothers and foolish. They were jealous of him and had had enough of his dreams that one day he would be over them. So they threw him into a pit intending to kill him, but by the Lord working through Judah and Reuben, Joseph's life was spared. He was sold into slavery instead. There he was lied about by the Potiphar's wife and put into prison. There he stayed until, by divine connection, the baker and the cupbearer and angered Pharaoh and were also thrown into prison. While in prison, Joseph persevered without attitude. He gained favor which is why we can ascertain that he did not have a poor attitude. "But while Joseph was there in the prison, the Lord was with him; he showed him kindness and granted him favor in the eyes of the prison warden. So the warden put Joseph in charge of all those held in the prison, and he was made responsible for all that was done there. The warden paid no attention to anything under Joseph's care, because the Lord was with Joseph and gave him success in whatever he did." (Genesis 39:20-23) A long trial and in those days I am quite certain the prison cells did not have all the comforts of home. He learned, he had a long time to learn through all he had been through and had grown up and in the favor of God. He was about to be delivered. While there, the baker and the cupbearer both had a dream.

Genesis 40—Joseph, the Baker and the Cupbearer

"Some time later, the cupbearer and the baker of the king of Egypt offended their master, the king of Egypt. Pharaoh was angry with his two officials, the chief cupbearer and the chief baker, and put them in custody in the house of the captain of the guard, in the same prison where Joseph was confined. The captain of the guard assigned them to Joseph, and he attended them.

After they had been in custody for some time, each of the two men—the cupbearer and the baker of the king of Egypt, who were being held in prison—had a dream the same night, and each dream had a meaning of its own. When Joseph came to them the next morning, he saw that they were dejected. So he asked Pharaoh's officials who were in custody with him in his master's house, "Why do you look so sad today?" "We both had dreams," they answered, "but there is no one to interpret them." Then Joseph said to them, "Do not interpretations belong to God? Tell me your dreams."

So the chief cupbearer told Joseph his dream. He said to him, "In my dream I saw a vine in front of me, and on the vine were three branches. As soon as it budded, it blossomed, and its clusters ripened into grapes. Pharaoh's cup was in my hand, and I took the grapes, squeezed them into Pharaoh's cup and put the cup in his hand." "This is what it means," Joseph said to him. "The three branches are three days. Within three days Pharaoh will lift up your head and restore you to your position, and you will put Pharaoh's cup in his hand, just as you used to do when you were his cupbearer. But when all goes well with you, remember me and show me kindness; mention me to Pharaoh and get me out of this prison. I was forcibly carried off from the land of the Hebrews, and even here I have done nothing to deserve being put in a dungeon."

When the chief baker saw that Joseph had given a favorable interpretation, he said to Joseph, "I too had a dream: On my head were three baskets of bread. In the top basket were all kinds of baked goods for Pharaoh, but the birds were eating them out of the basket on my head." "This is what it means," Joseph said. "The three baskets are three days. Within three days Pharaoh will lift off your head and impale your body on a pole. And the birds will eat away your flesh."

Now the third day was Pharaoh's birthday, and he gave a feast for all his officials. He lifted up the heads of the chief cupbearer and the chief baker in the presence of his officials: He restored the chief cupbearer to his position, so that he once again put the cup into Pharaoh's hand—but he impaled the chief baker, just as Joseph had said to them in his interpretation. The chief cupbearer, however, did not remember Joseph; he forgot him."

Continue reading Genesis 41-45. As a result of the baker and the cupbearer's dream, what happened? How long did it take before the rewards of Joseph interpreting their dreams correctly take?

_____

_____

_____

_____

_____

_____

_____

_____

_____

_____

_____

_____

_____

_____

Joseph spent a long time, a very long and difficult trial with many hardships for doing nothing. He stayed faithful and was promoted to the palace! What a reward! Two other things happened to the people of the country and to him and his family as a result of his faith, obedience and perseverance. What were they?

_____

_____

_____

_____

_____

_____

_____

_____

_____

_____

_____

_____

_____

_____

What have you learned through some of the trials you have been through? How has that changed your faith and your relationship with God?

_____

_____

_____

_____

_____

_____

_____

_____

_____

_____

Sandra Lott

Facebook Connect: Post to the FB some of the many things you have learned through the trials you have been through.

Chapter 9

Stepping Out

There is absolutely no way of drawing closer to God if you will not allow Him to live out His heart through you; if you will not step out of your comfort zone to be His vessel. Jesus came and left His Holy Spirit with us in order to give us what we need to live a victorious life both personally and as His ambassadors. An ambassador represents a country, and as a child of God, we are to represent Jesus Christ. "We are therefore Christ's ambassadors, as though God were making his appeal through us. We implore you on Christ's behalf: Be reconciled to God." (II Corinthians 5:20)

You cannot say you love God if you do not love people and show compassion for others. Because that is who God is, He is love. "If I speak in the tongues of men or of angels, but do not have love, I am only a resounding gong or a clanging cymbal. If I have the gift of prophecy and can fathom all mysteries and all knowledge, and if I have a faith that can move mountains, but do not have love, I am nothing. If I give all I possess to the poor and give over my body to hardship that I may boast, but do not have love, I gain nothing. Love is patient, love is kind. It does not envy, it does not boast, it is not proud. It does not dishonor others, it is not self-seeking, it is not easily angered, it keeps no record of wrongs. Love does not delight in evil but rejoices with the truth. It always protects, always trusts, always hopes, always perseveres. Love never fails. But where there are prophecies, they will cease; where there are tongues, they will be stilled; where there is knowledge, it will pass away. For we know in part and we prophesy in part, but when completeness comes, what is in part disappears. When I was a child, I talked like a child, I thought like a child, I reasoned like a child. When I became a man, I put the ways of childhood behind me. For now we see only a reflection as in a mirror; then we shall see face to face. Now I know in part; then I shall know fully, even as I am fully known. And now these three remain: faith, hope and love. But the greatest of these is love." (I Corinthians 13)

Love steps out, love takes action. Where would we all be if Jesus did not step out of His comfort zone for us? "Dear children, let us not love with words or speech but with actions and in truth." (I John 3:18)

Read the poems below and allow them to speak to you. There are many ways that you show the love of God and in doing so, His love touches others through you and you are bringing glory to His name.

Light of Jesus

Let the light of Jesus shine in your heart
let His love show in your daily walk.
Your faith will shine through, and the
power of God and all His glory will
overflow to one another.

By the love and faith that you show
you might help a hurting soul
and pass on the light of Jesus
to shine from your heart to theirs.
Just let His light shine and pass it on!

The Cross

Love comes in many ways,
a small babe in its mother's arms,
a gold band on the 3rd left finger
of two lover's hands.

Love comes in many ways,
When a small boy gives his last
dollar to an old man on the street,
when you give what you have, time,
possessions or money, to show that

Love comes in many ways,
When you risk your life to save

that of another, but the best way
of all is shown by the blood that
dripped down His face when He
hung on the cross to give us
everlasting grace.

Did You Reflect God's Glory Today?

Are you reflecting the glory of God? How did you look
at that homeless man you passed on the street? Did you
smile with the love of Jesus shining through or did you
give him a look of disgust as you walked past? Did you
reflect God's glory today? Have you let your light shine
before men, that they may see your good deeds and praise
your Father in heaven?

As you hurried to the next business meeting or errand
on your busy schedule today, how did you answer that one
that dared stop you to ask for a dollar? Did you reflect the
glory of God or did you ignore him, passing by with a look
of irritation on your face? Don't you know what you do to
the least of these brothers you do unto Jesus Christ
Himself?

Have you reflected the glory of God today? As you
hurried by to the next errand of the day, how did you treat
that one that stopped you; who was lost and confused and
needed directions? Did you let your light shine giving glory

to God? Or did you snap at them with total impatience making them feel as low as the dirt beneath your feet? Did they see Jesus in you?

Have you reflected God's glory today? In the midst of your day as you passed that one crying on a nearby bench, did you stop and offer a shoulder to cry on just as Jesus still does for you? Did you offer to pray with them being the witness you should be? Did you reflect the glory of God or did you just pass him by as if he was nothing? You had more important things to do. Where would we all be if Jesus thought that way on the road to Calvary? Yet we are all something to Him. He died for us. Is our day and our plans much more important than His? Don't you know, the Father of compassion and the God of all comfort, comforts us in all our troubles, so that we can comfort those in any trouble with the comfort we ourselves have received from God?

Did you reflect God's glory today? Have you let your light shine before men that they may praise God? Were you Jesus to the world today? Have you made a difference in someone's life today? Were you a blessing and maybe the only Jesus that they may see?

If not, then remember this Scripture from Hebrews 4:13, "Nothing in all creation is hidden from God's sight. Everything is uncovered and laid bare before the eyes of Him to whom we must give account."

Did you reflect God's glory and was He pleased with you today? Is your life and example of God's love and His glory? Or are you breaking the third commandment and misusing the name of the Lord your God by what you say, the way you live and how you treat others? Did you reflect God's glory today?

There are many ways to show the love of God. You can smile at that neighbor or coworker that just rubs you the wrong way. You can go out of your way to give someone a ride. You can lend a helping hand at church or volunteer at a shelter or nursing home. There are many ways. As you read through these poems did you find more ways to step out of your comfort zone?

_____

_____

_____

_____

_____

_____

_____

_____

_____

_____

_____

_____

_____

_____

Genesis 12:1-9--Abram (Abraham) Gets Called by God & to Leave Home

"The Lord had said to Abram, "Go from your country, your people and your father's household to the land I will show you. "I will make you into a great nation, and I will bless you; I will make your name great, and you will be a blessing. I will bless those who bless you, and whoever curses you I will curse; and all peoples on earth will be blessed through you." So Abram went, as the Lord had told him; and Lot went with him. Abram was seventy-five years old when he set out from Harran. He took his wife Sarai, his nephew Lot, all the possessions they had accumulated and the people they had acquired in Harran, and they set out for the land of Canaan, and they arrived there. Abram traveled through the land as far as the site of the great tree of Moreh at Shechem. At that time the Canaanites were in the land. The Lord appeared to Abram and said, "To your offspring. I will give this land." So he built an altar there to the Lord, who had appeared to him. From there he went on toward the hills east of Bethel and pitched his tent, with Bethel on the west and Ai on the east. There he built an altar to the Lord and called on the name of the Lord. Then Abram set out and continued toward the Negev."

God called Abram to leave his country and what he knew to be his home and family to a distant country. I would call that a bit out of his comfort zone. He obeyed. What were the promises for his obedience? How did his obedience help everyone who calls themselves a child of God?

_____

_____

_____

_____

_____

_____

_____

_____

_____

_____

_____

_____

_____

_____

Has God been calling you to step out of your comfort zone? Have you listened? How can your obedience help spread the Word of God? How can it help others and in doing so give glory to God? Need help? Not sure? Pray and ask the Holy Spirit to reveal new and inspired ways to show the love of God.

_____

_____

_____

_____

_____

_____

_____

_____

_____

_____

_____

_____

_____

_____

_____

_____

_____

_____

_____

_____

_____

_____

_____

_____

_____

_____

Sandra Lott

Facebook Connect: Post to the FB page the inspirations God has spoken to your heart as you read through this devotion. Has He given you any new ways you can step out and be His heart?

Chapter 10
Dunked!

If you have not been baptized in the Holy Spirit, then pray and ask for it! This is one part of being a child of God that you do not want miss out on. There is one Spirit, and One baptism and Jesus told the disciples to wait for it. He told them to wait before going out in the world to be His apostles until they received the baptism.

"In my former book, Theophilus, I wrote about all that Jesus began to do and to teach until the day He was taken up to heaven, after giving instructions through the Holy Spirit to the apostles He had chosen. After His suffering, He presented Himself to them and gave many convincing proofs that He was alive. He appeared to them over a period of forty days and spoke about the kingdom of God. On one occasion, while He was eating with them, He gave them this command: "Do not leave Jerusalem, but wait for the gift My Father promised, which you have heard Me speak about. For John baptized with water, but in a few days you will be baptized with the Holy Spirit." Then they gathered around Him and asked Him, "Lord, are you at this time going to restore the kingdom to Israel?" He said to them: "It is not for you to know the times or dates the Father has set by His own authority. But you will receive power when the Holy Spirit comes on you; and you will be My witnesses in Jerusalem, and in all Judea and Samaria, and to the ends of the earth." After He said this, He was taken up before their very eyes, and a cloud hid Him from their sight." (Acts 1:1-9)

You are filled with the Holy Spirit upon conversion, but being baptized with the Holy Spirit is like being dunked! You are totally immersed in the Holy Spirit. He will also give you gifts, and some of you may have all, or just some. It is according to how He gives them and according to the purpose God has for you. "For we are God's handiwork, created in Christ Jesus to do good works, which God prepared in advance for us to do." (Ephesians 2:10)

"Now about the gifts of the Spirit, brothers and sisters, I do not want you to be uninformed. You know that when you were pagans, somehow or other you were influenced and led astray to mute idols. Therefore I want you to know that no one who is speaking by the Spirit of God says, "Jesus be cursed," and no one can say, "Jesus is Lord," except by the Holy Spirit. There are different kinds of gifts, but the same Spirit distributes them. There are different kinds of service, but the same Lord. There are different kinds of working, but in all of them and in everyone it is the same God at work. Now to each one the manifestation of the Spirit is given for the common good. To one there is given through the Spirit a message of **wisdom,** to another a **message of knowledge** by means of the same Spirit, to another **faith** by the same Spirit, to another **gifts of healing** by that one Spirit, to another **miraculous powers**, to another **prophecy**, to **another distinguishing between spirits**, to another **speaking in different kinds of tongues**, and to still another the **interpretation of tongues**. All these are the work of one and the same Spirit, and he distributes them to each one, just as he determines." I Corinthians 12:1-11)

There gifts of office for His purpose, "So Christ Himself gave the apostles, the prophets, the evangelists, the pastors and teachers, to equip the saints for works of ministry, to build up the body of Christ. (Ephesians 4:11-12)

It is not something to be afraid of but desired and cherished. The Holy Spirit is gentle and as you ask, He will give in His time and His way. Everyone is different and how He immerses you in Himself will be special for you. "So I say to you: Ask and it will be given to you; seek and you will find; knock and the door will be opened to you. For everyone who asks receives; the one who seeks finds; and to the one who knocks, the door will be opened.

"Which of you fathers, if your son asks for a fish, will give him a snake instead? Or if he asks for an egg, will give him a scorpion? If you then, though you are evil, know how to give good gifts to your children, how much more will your Father in heaven give the Holy Spirit to those who ask Him!" (Luke 11:9-13) I go into more detail into the Baptism of Holy Spirit in my book: The Holy Spirit and the Baptism of the Holy Spirit.

Peter had denied the Lord three times; Jesus even told him before the Roman soldiers took Him away that he would. He said that the devil desired to "sift him," but He would pray for Him. Peter messed up, he did deny Jesus and then felt horrible afterward. But when Jesus rose from the dead and Peter heard, oh, the life of Jesus that He brings to your spirit. It renewed him, and he preached on that Pentecost following.

Acts 2:1-41—Peter Preached on Pentecost after being Baptized

"When the day of Pentecost came, they were all together in one place. Suddenly a sound like the blowing of a violent wind came from heaven and filled the whole house where they were sitting. They saw what seemed to be tongues of fire that separated and came to rest on each of them. All of them were filled with the Holy Spirit and began to speak in other tongues as the Spirit enabled them. Now there were staying in Jerusalem God-fearing Jews from every nation under heaven. When they heard this sound, a crowd came together in bewilderment, because each one heard their own language being spoken. Utterly amazed, they asked: "Aren't all these who are speaking Galileans? Then how is it that each of us hears them in our native language? Parthians, Medes and Elamites; residents of Mesopotamia, Judea and Cappadocia, Pontus and Asia, Phrygia and Pamphylia, Egypt and the parts of Libya near Cyrene; visitors from Rome (both Jews and converts to Judaism); Cretans and Arabs—we hear them declaring the wonders of God in our own tongues!" Amazed and perplexed, they asked one another, "What does this mean?" Some, however, made fun of them and said, "They have had too much wine."

Peter Addresses the Crowd

Then Peter stood up with the Eleven, raised his voice and addressed the crowd: "Fellow Jews and all of you who live in Jerusalem, let me explain this to you; listen carefully to what I say. These people are not drunk, as you suppose. It's only nine in the morning! No, this is what was spoken by the prophet Joel: " 'In the last days, God says, I will pour out My Spirit on all people. Your sons and daughters will prophesy, your young men will see visions, your old men will dream dreams. Even on My servants, both men and women, I will pour out My Spirit in those days, and they will prophesy. I will show wonders in the heavens above and signs on the earth below, blood and fire and billows of smoke. The sun will be turned to darkness and the moon to blood before the coming of the great and glorious day of the Lord. And everyone who calls on the name of the Lord will be saved.' "Fellow Israelites, listen to this: Jesus of Nazareth was a man accredited by God to you by miracles, wonders and signs, which God did among you through Him, as you yourselves know. This man was handed over to you by God's deliberate plan and foreknowledge; and you, with the help of wicked men, put Him to death by nailing Him to the cross. But God raised Him from the dead, freeing him from the agony of death, because it was impossible for death to keep its hold on

Him. David said about Him: " 'I saw the Lord always before me. Because He is at my right hand, I will not be shaken. Therefore my heart is glad and my tongue rejoices; my body also will rest in hope, because you will not abandon me to the realm of the dead, you will not let your holy one see decay. You have made known to me the paths of life; You will fill me with joy in Your presence.' "Fellow Israelites, I can tell you confidently that the patriarch David died and was buried, and his tomb is here to this day. But he was a prophet and knew that God had promised him on oath that he would place one of his descendants on his throne. Seeing what was to come, he spoke of the resurrection of the Messiah, that He was not abandoned to the realm of the dead, nor did His body see decay. God has raised this Jesus to life, and we are all witnesses of it. Exalted to the right hand of God, He has received from the Father the promised Holy Spirit and has poured out what you now see and hear. For David did not ascend to heaven, and yet he said, " 'The Lord said to my Lord: "Sit at my right hand until I make Your enemies a footstool for Your feet." ' "Therefore let all Israel be assured of this: God has made this Jesus, whom you crucified, both Lord and Messiah." When the people heard this, they were cut to the heart and said to Peter and the other apostles, "Brothers, what shall we do?" Peter replied, "Repent and be baptized, every one of you, in the name of Jesus Christ for the forgiveness of your sins. And you will receive the gift of the Holy Spirit. The promise is for you and your children and for all who are far off—for all whom the Lord our God will call." With many other words He warned them; and He pleaded with them, "Save yourselves from this corrupt generation." Those who accepted his message were baptized, and about three thousand were added to their number that day."

Peter had denied Jesus three times but returned and was forgiven and was baptized in the Holy Spirit. He preached on that first Pentecost after the death of Jesus. What happened on that first Pentecost? How was each of the apostles speaking? How many people were affected? How many more people in your everyday life that you see at work, at home, in your family, your neighborhood, at the store and at church can God show Himself to through you and even more if you were baptized in the Holy Spirit?

_____

_____

_____

_____

_____

_____

_____

_____

_____

_____

_____

Being baptized in the Holy Spirit equips you with even more to be the Lord's vessel. You don't have to be perfect to receive, Peter is proof of that, you just need to ask. Signs will accompany, and do not allow the enemy to deceive you into thinking that you have not been baptized or that you are not speaking in tongues. If you ask, your surrender and worship in His presence, opening your mouth in praise, He will baptize you. It may take a couple of times, sometimes if you are fearful, it can get in the way, but keep asking, keep seeking it will happen. This is a step to intimacy that is vital if you want more of Him. "He said to them, "Go into all the world and preach the gospel to all creation. Whoever believes and is baptized will be saved, but whoever does not believe will be condemned. And these signs will accompany those who believe: In my name they will drive out demons; they will speak in new tongues; they will pick up snakes with their hands; and when they drink deadly poison, it will not hurt them at all; they will place their hands on sick people, and they will get well." After the Lord Jesus had spoken to them, He was taken up into heaven and He sat at the right hand of God. Then the disciples went out and preached everywhere, and the Lord worked with them and confirmed His word by the signs that accompanied it." (Mark 16:15-20)

If you have not received the baptism, ask. Speak to the Lord and tell Him your heart, ask Him to speak to you regarding this and record it below.

Sandra Lott

_____

_____

_____

_____

_____

_____

_____

_____

_____

_____

_____

_____

_____

_____

_____

_____

_____

Facebook Connect: Post to the FB if you have been baptized in the Holy Spirit and the difference it has made in your Christian walk. If you have not, post any new revelations the Holy Spirit revealed to you about being baptized.

Chapter 11
Deeper Still

We have covered a lot and by now my prayer is that all of this has truly drawn you closer and closer to God. But there is still more, yes more. In chapter 4 we talked about the necessity of developing a good prayer life. Well, communication is two-way. There talking and listening. It is easy to get the talking part down but listening, sometimes that is not always easy to do. Everyone is different and there is no one special way to quiet your mind in order to listen to the Lord speak to your heart and God wants to speak! "For God does speak--now one way, now another-- though no one perceives it. In a dream, in a vision of the night, when deep sleep falls on people as they slumber in their beds, He may speak in their ears and terrify them with warnings, to preserve them from the pit, their lives from perishing by the sword." (Job 33:14-18)

God wants to talk to you, but it is hard to hear through all the clamor of your mind sometimes. "Be still before the Lord, all mankind, because He has roused Himself from His holy dwelling." (Zechariah 2:13) When you make the effort to seek Him, you will find Him, you will hear Him, He wants to speak. "I love those who love Me, and those who seek Me find Me." (Proverbs 8:17)

So, you need to learn a way that works for you how to quiet your mind. Most people, I have found quiet their mind with quiet worship music. "Enter His gates with thanksgiving and His courts with praise; give thanks to Him and praise His Name." (Psalm 100:4) Think about it, Satan used to be the worship leader so to speak in heaven, and he left it! Do you think he wants to stick around and praise God with you? He may try for a while, but after you continue, press past the flesh, all the emotions and things going through your mind, as you continue in worship and focus on Him, your mind will quiet. But for others, it is turning off everything and there is still trouble, examining yourself to see if there may be something you need to seek forgiveness for or give it.

God will make it personal to you and how you quiet your mind in order to listen to the Lord's still small voice is personal as well. For me, it is listening to quiet praise music, and getting alone with anything that I have to do, out of the way. Everything else can wait. The enemy will try to flood your mind with a list of "need to do's," but push it out of your mind. How you choose to do that is also a personal thing. One person told me they keep a notepad close by and jot whatever comes to mind down on it and then go back to their quiet time.

The way He speaks to you is personal as well. He may speak to you while doing something, watching your children or your pets playing, or birds in the air or maybe just taking in the sun outside. Something will come into your mind or you are suddenly reminded of a verse. He may speak to you while you're doing everyday things like going to the store, and something catches your attention, or someone says something, and a light goes off! Yes, that is what God is trying to tell me! It may be while in church a word is said, and it speaks to your heart or while you are praising His name. You could be driving down the road and suddenly inspired. It will be just what you needed to hear. When He does speak directly to your heart, you will know it, it will be with a sense of peace and a warmth in your heart. "They asked each other, "Were not our hearts burning within us while he talked with us on the road and opened the Scriptures to us?" (Luke 24:32) When you are led by the Spirit, you will know it is Him. "For those who are led by the Spirit of God are the children of God. The Spirit you received does not make you slaves, so that you live in fear again; rather, the Spirit you received brought about your adoption to sonship. And by Him, we cry, "Abba, Father." The Spirit Himself testifies with our spirit that we are God's children. Now if we are children, then we are heirs—heirs of God and co-heirs with Christ, if indeed we share in His sufferings in order that we may also share in His glory." (Romans 8:14-17)

He may speak through trials as well. In the days of the Judges, the Israelites had allowed the gods of the people of the land into their homes. God told them to destroy all the peoples of the land upon entering the Promised Land and they did not obey. Treaties and intermarrying resulted, and they became lax in their devotion to God. They slowly slipped away from obeying Him. That is the way the enemy works, he desensitizes us into thinking, "oh that is not too bad," and before long you get further and further away from God. This is what happened to the Israelites and God had to get their attention in order to get them back on the right path with Him. He did that in Judges 6 by the oppression of the Midianites and the Amalekites. Sometimes allowing the trials are the only way He can get us to cry out to Him. He not only allowed the trial, but He, Himself as an Angel of the Lord showed up to Gideon. He provided the answer! But in the answer to go up against them, He dwindled the army down from 32,000 to 300 fighting men. And He used Gideon who was full of fear. He used the weakest tribe and a man who himself was full of fear and talking the Lord, new He was of God and destroyed the altars to the false gods, he still gave into fear and fleeced the Lord twice!

Judges 7--God Reduces the Army

"Early in the morning, Jerub-Baal (that is, Gideon) and all his men camped at the spring of Harod. The camp of Midian was north of them in the valley near the hill of Moreh. The Lord said to Gideon, "You have too many men. I cannot deliver Midian into their hands, or Israel would boast against me, 'My own strength has saved me.' Now announce to the army, 'Anyone who trembles with fear may turn back and leave Mount Gilead.'" So, twenty-two thousand men left, while ten thousand remained. But the Lord said to Gideon, "There are still too many men.

Take them down to the water, and I will thin them out for you there. If I say, 'This one shall go with you,' he shall go; but if I say, 'This one shall not go with you,' he shall not go."

So, Gideon took the men down to the water. There the Lord told him, "Separate those who lap the water with their tongues as a dog laps from those who kneel down to drink." Three hundred of them drank from cupped hands, lapping like dogs. All the rest got down on their knees to drink. The Lord said to Gideon, "With the three hundred men that lapped I will save you and give the Midianites into your hands. Let all the others go home." So, Gideon sent the rest of the Israelites home but kept the three hundred, who took over the provisions and trumpets of the others. Now the camp of Midian lay below him in the valley during that night the Lord said to Gideon, "Get up, go down against the camp, because I am going to give it into your hands.

If you are afraid to attack, go down to the camp with your servant Purah and listen to what they are saying. Afterward, you will be encouraged to attack the camp." So, he and Purah his servant went down to the outposts of the camp. The Midianites, the Amalekites and all the other eastern peoples had settled in the valley, thick as locusts. Their camels could no more be counted than the sand on the seashore. Gideon arrived just as a man was telling a friend his dream. "I had a dream," he was saying. "A round loaf of barley bread came tumbling into the Midianite camp. It struck the tent with such force that the tent overturned and collapsed." His friend responded, "This can be nothing other than the sword of Gideon son of Joash, the Israelite. God has given the Midianites and the whole camp into his hands." When Gideon heard the dream and its interpretation, he bowed down and worshiped. He returned to the camp of Israel and called out, "Get up! The Lord has given the Midianite camp into your hands." Dividing the three hundred men into three companies, he placed trumpets and empty jars in the hands of all of them, with torches inside.

Watch me," he told them. "Follow my lead. When I get to the edge of the camp, do exactly as I do. When I and all who are with me blow our trumpets, then from all around the camp blow yours and shout, 'For the Lord and for Gideon.'" Gideon and the hundred men with him reached the edge of the camp at the beginning of the middle watch, just after they had changed the guard. They blew their trumpets and broke the jars that were in their hands. The three companies blew the trumpets and smashed the jars. Grasping the torches in their left hands and holding in their right hands the trumpets they were to blow, they shouted, "A sword for the Lord and for Gideon!" While each man held his position around the camp, all the Midianites ran, crying out as they fled. When the three hundred trumpets sounded, the Lord caused the men throughout the camp to turn on each other with their swords. The army fled to Beth Shittah toward Zererah as far as the border of Abel Meholah near Tabbath. Israelites from Naphtali, Asher and all Manasseh were called out, and they pursued the Midianites. Gideon sent messengers throughout the hill country of Ephraim, saying, "Come down against the Midianites and seize the waters of the Jordan ahead of them as far as Beth Barah." So, all the men of Ephraim were called out and they seized the waters of the Jordan as far as Beth Barah. They also captured two of the Midianite leaders, Oreb and Zeeb. They killed Oreb at the rock of Oreb, and Zeeb at the winepress of Zeeb. They pursued the Midianites and brought the heads of Oreb and Zeeb to Gideon, who was by the Jordan."

Why did God reduce the army to 300 men? Look at your life and the trials you went through. Has God ever had to reduce what you had in order to show Himself mighty to you? Record those moments below as a remembrance to give you hope in the next trial.

_____

_____

_____

_____

_____

_____

_____

_____

_____

_____

God may speak through the Word or a passage may catch your attention as if it illuminated. "All Scripture is God-breathed and is useful for teaching, rebuking, correcting and training in righteousness, so that the man of God may be complete, fully equipped for every good work." (II Timothy 3:16-17) A verse may come to your mind or it may seem as if someone just whispered something, a phrase, something to do, an inspiration, into your ear.

"The Lord said, "Go out and stand on the mountain in the presence of the Lord, for the Lord is about to pass by." Then a great and powerful wind tore the mountains apart and shattered the rocks before the Lord, but the Lord was not in the wind. After the wind there was an earthquake, but the Lord was not in the earthquake. After the earthquake came a fire, but the Lord was not in the fire. And after the fire came a gentle whisper." (I Kings 19:11-12)

He may give you a picture in your mind or even something more personal that will speak specifically to you. For example, when my oldest son had accepted the Lord as Savior, He told me through my writing. I did not get it until the next day. He gave me a poem one Saturday evening called, Mama on Her Knees. It did not register with me at the time. My son was going to church with me and we were going in his car. He usually listened to a heavy metal radio station. So, we got in the car and he turned on the radio and my eyes lit up! It was on a Christian radio

station! A light bulb went off and I got it, that is what God was trying to tell me. My son was saved!
"Listen to my words: "When there is a prophet among you, I, the Lord, reveal myself to them in visions, I speak to them in dreams." (Numbers 12:6)

God Speaks

In the whispers of the wind and

the still small voice within your heart

God speaks to you and me.

His love is like the quiet ripples of a river
flowing gently through your heart
keeping you in perfect peace within.

As the leaves rustle when the wind blows through
you can hear God speak to me and you.

With every smile and "I love you" that you share
whether it's the words that you say or the
helping hand that shows that you care,
God speaks.

The mountains sitting proud and tall
tell of God's power and might.

In the seas with the waters flowing on and on
their end is nowhere in sight,
God speaks of His love. It's like a river
flowing through your heart.

Abounding like the seas, is His love which
in the Holy Spirit He speaks to you and me.
In His power and might and the beauty of the world,
God speaks.

As in the never-ending seas, His love flows on and on.
God speaks. In the blood He shed on Calvary.
God Speaks.

He's telling you "He loves you" and if
you believe and receive He'll make
your heart eternally brand new.

On the pages of His Word, in the whispers of the wind
and the ripples of the sea, His Holy Spirit is there, and
He speaks to you and me.

Acts 10:1-23

"At Caesarea, there was a man named Cornelius, a
centurion in what was known as the Italian Regiment. He
and all his family were devout and God-fearing; he gave

generously to those in need and prayed to God regularly. One day at about three in the afternoon he had a vision. He distinctly saw an angel of God, who came to him and said, "Cornelius!" Cornelius stared at him in fear. "What is it, Lord?" he asked.

The angel answered, "Your prayers and gifts to the poor have come up as a memorial offering before God. Now send men to Joppa to bring back a man named Simon who is called Peter. He is staying with Simon the tanner; whose house is by the sea."

When the angel who spoke to him had gone, Cornelius called two of his servants and a devout soldier who was one of his attendants. He told them everything that had happened and sent them to Joppa."

Peter's Vision

"About noon the following day as they were on their journey and approaching the city, Peter went up on the roof to pray. He became hungry and wanted something to eat, and while the meal was being prepared, he fell into a trance. He saw heaven opened and something like a large sheet being let down to earth by its four corners. It contained all kinds of four-footed animals, as well as reptiles and birds. Then a voice told him, "Get up, Peter. Kill and eat." "Surely not, Lord!" Peter replied. "I have never eaten anything impure or unclean." The voice spoke to him a second time, "Do not call anything impure that God has made clean." This happened three times, and immediately the sheet was taken back to heaven. While Peter was wondering about the meaning of the vision, the men sent by Cornelius found out where Simon's house was and stopped at the gate. They called out, asking if Simon who was known as Peter was staying there. While Peter was still thinking about the vision, the Spirit said to him, "Simon, three men are looking for you. So, get up and go downstairs. Do not hesitate to go with them, for I have sent them." Peter went down and said to the men, "I'm the one you're looking for. Why have you come?" The men replied, "We have come from Cornelius the centurion. He is a righteous and God-fearing man, who is respected by all the Jewish people. A holy angel told him to ask you to come to his house so that he could hear what you have to say." Then Peter invited the men into the house to be his guests."

In Leviticus 11:26-27 the Lord said that all animals that are hooved with split but not divided hooves and four-footed animals that walk on their paws were unclean. There were issues arising between the Jewish people and the disciples about people receiving the Lord. The Lord was trying to make it clear that all men, not just the Jewish people, who called on the name of the Lord would be saved. He gave him a vision in order to make His point clear.

Today what does this represent? Are there any areas in your life that you have found yourself to have issues regarding this? Record your comments, thoughts, and prayers below.

_____

_____

_____

_____

_____

_____

_____

_____

_____

_____

_____

_____

"For I know the plans I have for you," declares the Lord, "plans to prosper you and not to harm you, plans to give you hope and a future. Then you will call on me and come and pray to me, and I will listen to you. You will seek me and find me when you seek me with all your heart. I will be found by you," declares the Lord, "and will bring you back from captivity." (Jeremiah 29:11-14)

You will hear from God when you take the time to listen. Pray and ask the Lord to help you if you struggle in this area. And being a child of God, you will know His voice, the peace that comes with it. "My sheep hear My voice, and I know them, and they follow Me." (John 10:27) Being able to talk and listen to God is so rewarding. Think about it, God Almighty, creator of all mankind and He wants to have a personal one on one relationship with us. Meditate on the words of this chapter and allow the Holy Spirit to give you a fresh revelation of Himself. Record it below.

_____

_____

_____

_____

_____

_____

_____

_____

_____

_____

_____

Sandra Lott

_____

_____

_____

_____

_____

_____

_____

_____

_____

_____

_____

_____

_____

_____

_____

_____

_____

Facebook Connect: Post to the FB some of the many things you have learned through about taking time to listen to God.

Chapter 12
Give Thanks

$\mathcal{I}$have been through some very difficult times in my life from my personal relationships, and continually making some huge blunders that have cost me, to losing my sixteen-year-old son to a car accident. That was the darkest time in my life and honestly, I wanted to go with him. I was numb for weeks. My heart was shattered into pieces and God kept every piece and glued it back together. Ironically enough, after Gerald Ray's death, God gave me my first book to write called: God's love. It is about the many different facets of His love from creation, the Bible, His mercy and compassion, His faithfulness, His protection, salvation, Jesus, the Holy Spirit and more. God took a piece of my heart home to be with Him, but with every word He gave me to write then, and continues to give me to write now, He gives a part of it back. There are analogies of my son, and my mother, who I also lost while writing that book exactly two years after my son died. Through it all I can say I am so thankful for God and our Lord and Savior Jesus Christ.

In this world we will have trouble, unfortunately; we live in a fallen world full of evil. So, it does not matter who you are, you are going to experience hard times and I would rather do it as a child of God. "I have told you these things, so that in me you may have peace. In this world you will have trouble. But take heart! I have overcome the world." (John 16:33) He gives me strength whenever I need it, He gives me grace, grace and more grace and when I fall, He is always faithful to pick me up. "The Lord is trustworthy in all He promises and faithful in all He does. The Lord upholds all who fall and lifts up all who are bowed down." (Psalm 145:13-14)

I am thankful for Jesus Christ and the salvation of my soul by His death and resurrection. If not for Him and His unconditional love, the blood He shed on the cross, my eternal home as well as everyone else would not be in heaven. I am thankful for the Holy Spirit, through Him, I am reminded of verses right when I need them. He gives me hope and encouragement and fills my heart with peace. "Peace I leave with you; My peace I give to you. I do not give to you as the world gives. Do not let your hearts be troubled; do not be afraid." (John 14:27) He gives me wisdom when I need an answer and when I feel alone, through the Holy Spirit I feel the overwhelming love of God. "When the Comforter comes, whom I will send to you from the Father—the Spirit of truth who goes out from the Father—He will testify about Me." (John 15:26)

Just like the many different names that make up who He is, God is all you need. I am thankful for His mercy and

compassion. I have needed it over and over and He still shows it continually. "Because of the Lord's great love, we are not consumed, for His compassions never fail. They are new every morning; great is Your faithfulness.
I say to myself, "The Lord is my portion; therefore, I will wait for Him." The Lord is good to those whose hope is in Him, to the one who seeks Him; it is good to wait quietly for the salvation of the Lord." (Lamentations 3;22-26)

Having an attitude of thanksgiving, even in your darkest times keeps your heart focused on God. "Rejoice always, pray continually, give thanks in all circumstances; for this is God's will for you in Christ Jesus. Do not quench the Spirit. Do not treat prophecies with contempt but test them all; hold on to what is good, reject every kind of evil. May God Himself, the God of peace, sanctify you through and through. May your whole spirit, soul and body be kept blameless at the coming of our Lord Jesus Christ. The one who calls you is faithful, and he will do it." (I Thessalonians 5:16-24)

There is always something to be thankful for, you have to take your eyes off of yourself and your problems long enough to see. Do you have a place to live and food to eat? Some people are homeless and without food. What about your health, or having all the parts of your body? Do you have a family? Some people are all alone in the world. What about clean water? Some people only have the water they find in dirty ravines. Being thankful and having an attitude of gratitude leaves no room for the devil to creep into your heart. You leave a crack, he will widen it and take it all! Keeping a thankful heart, keeps your eyes focused on God and keeps the devil out! "That, however; is not the way of life you learned when you heard about Christ and were taught in him in accordance with the truth that is in Jesus. You were taught, with regard to your former way of life, to put off your old self, which is being corrupted by its deceitful desires; to be made new in the attitude of your minds; and to put on the new self, created to be like God in true righteousness and holiness. Therefore, each of you must put off falsehood and speak truthfully to your neighbor, for we are all members of one body. "In your anger do not sin": Do not let the sun go down while you are still angry, and do not give the devil a foothold." (Ephesians 4:20-27)

So, you see, if you look you can find many things to be thankful for and the best one of all, is your salvation and the ability to talk to God Almighty, Creator of heaven and earth and not only be heard but get an answer back!

Daniel 6—Daniel Give thanks Anyway

"It pleased Darius to appoint 120 satraps to rule throughout the kingdom, with three administrators over them, one of whom was Daniel. The satraps were made accountable to them so that the king might not suffer loss. Now Daniel so distinguished himself among the administrators and the satraps by his exceptional qualities that the king planned to set him over the whole kingdom. At this, the administrators and the satraps tried to find grounds for charges against Daniel in his conduct of government affairs, but they were unable to do so. They could find no corruption in him, because he was trustworthy and neither corrupt nor negligent. Finally these men said, "We will never find any basis for charges against this man Daniel unless it has something to do with the law of his God."

So, these administrators and satraps went as a group to the king and said: "May King Darius live forever! The royal administrators, prefects, satraps, advisers and governors have all agreed that the king should issue an edict and enforce the decree that anyone who prays to any God or human being during the next thirty days, except to you, Your Majesty, shall be thrown into the lions' den. Now, Your Majesty, issue the decree and put it in writing so that it cannot be altered—in accordance with the law of the Medes and Persians, which cannot be repealed." So King Darius put the decree in writing.

Now when Daniel learned that the decree had been published, he went home to his upstairs room where the windows opened toward Jerusalem. Three times a day he got down on his knees and prayed, giving thanks to his God, just as he had done before. Then these men went as a group and found Daniel praying and asking God for help. So they went to the king and spoke to him about his royal decree: "Did you not publish a decree that during the next thirty days anyone who prays to any god or human being except to you, Your Majesty, would be thrown into the lions' den?"

The king answered, "The decree stands—in accordance with the law of the Medes and Persians, which cannot be repealed." Then they said to the king, "Daniel, who is one of the exiles from Judah, pays no attention to you, Your

Majesty, or to the decree you put in writing. He still prays three times a day." When the king heard this, he was greatly distressed; he was determined to rescue Daniel and made every effort until sundown to save him. Then the men went as a group to King Darius and said to him, "Remember, Your Majesty, that according to the law of the Medes and Persians no decree or edict that the king issues can be changed." So, the king gave the order, and they brought Daniel and threw him into the lions' den. The king said to Daniel, "May your God, whom you serve continually, rescue you!"

A stone was brought and placed over the mouth of the den, and the king sealed it with his own signet ring and with the rings of his nobles, so that Daniel's situation might not be changed. Then the king returned to his palace and spent the night without eating and without any entertainment being brought to him. And he could not sleep. At the first light of dawn, the king got up and hurried to the lions' den. When he came near the den, he called to Daniel in an anguished voice, "Daniel, servant of the living God, has your God, whom you serve continually, been able to rescue you from the lions?" Daniel answered, "May the king live forever! My God sent His angel, and He shut the mouths of the lions. They have not hurt me, because I was found innocent in His sight. Nor have I ever done any wrong before you, Your Majesty."

The king was overjoyed and gave orders to lift Daniel out of the den. And when Daniel was lifted from the den, no wound was found on him, because he had trusted in his God. At the king's command, the men who had falsely accused Daniel were brought in and thrown into the lions' den, along with their wives and children. And before they reached the floor of the den, the lions overpowered them and crushed all their bones. Then King Darius wrote to all the nations and peoples of every language in all the earth: "May you prosper greatly! "I issue a decree that in every part of my kingdom people must fear and reverence the God of Daniel. "For He is the living God and He endures forever; His kingdom will not be destroyed, His dominion will never end. He rescues, and He saves; He performs signs and wonders in the heavens and on the earth. He has rescued Daniel from the power of the lions." So Daniel prospered during the reign of Darius and the reign of Cyrus the Persian.

Daniel and his three friends were taken into the palace of Nebuchadnezzar king of Babylon when the Israelites were taken into captivity. Daniel and his friends through their integrity gained favor. Time passed and now the rule is under King Darius. Daniel still acted with integrity and King Darius planned to promote him. This did not go over to well with the administrators of the palace, so they planned to set him up. They knew he prayed to his God and set a trap. They talked King Darius into issuing a decree if anyone was to pray to anyone or anything other than the King, they would be thrown into the lion's den.

Learning this, what did Daniel continue to do? What happened as a result of his continued faithfulness to God?

_____

_____

_____

_____

_____

_____

_____

_____

_____

_____

_____

_____

_____

Your thanksgiving and your faithfulness to God makes a difference. People do see, and it makes a difference. "You are the light of the world. A town built on a hill cannot be hidden. Neither do people light a lamp and put it under a bowl. Instead they put it on its stand, and it gives light to everyone in the house. In the same way, let your light shine before others, that they may see your good deeds and glorify your Father in heaven." (Matthew 5:14-16)

Not only that, we are made in the image of God. He gave us emotions and enjoys our uniqueness, but just as we are made in His image and you read about His joy and His sadness in the Word, then the emotions we have came from Him. If we do not like to be used, misjudged, taken for granted, how do you think it makes Him feel?

Are you thankful? Do you thank God for the little things as well as the big things? Are your prayers full of needs and concerns, which are good and He wants to hear them, but do you thank Him as well? What are some things that you are thankful for? List them below as a prayer of thanksgiving to your Heavenly Father.

_____

_____

_____

_____

_____

_____

_____

_____

_____

_____

Sandra Lott

Facebook Connect: Post to the FB as a message to God and your thanks to Him in your daily life.

Final Thoughts

$\mathcal{I}$ hope by now that you have been saturated in the love of God as you read through this book. This devotional was meant to be taken slow and meditate on each topic and examine yourself along the way, allowing the Holy Spirit room to convict or give you a fresh revelation. Keep this book in reach and as you go through new trials read back on some of your comments, and see if you have new ones. Allow some of the remembrances you recorded to be an encouragement for new situations.

God wants an intimate relationship with each and every one of us. "I will give them a heart to know me, that I am the Lord. They will be My people, and I will be their God, for they will return to Me with all their heart." (Jeremiah 24:7) Keep seeking Him, you will be rewarded. "As the deer pants for streams of water, so my soul pants for you, my God. My soul thirsts for God, for the living God. When can I go and meet with God?" (Psalm 42:1-2)

As you keep seeking and become more and more intimate with Him, you become more and more sensitive to His Spirit. You are blessed in your sprit beyond measure and it will be displayed in your life as well. "Blessed is the one who does not walk in step with the wicked or stand in the way that sinners take or sit in the company of mockers, but whose delight is in the law of the Lord, and who meditates on his law, day and night. That person is like a tree planted by streams of water, which yields its fruit in season and whose leaf does not wither—whatever they do prospers. Not so the wicked! They are like chaff that the wind blows away. Therefore, the wicked will not stand in the judgment, nor sinners in the assembly of the righteous. For the Lord watches over the way of the righteous, but the way of the wicked leads to destruction." (Psalm 1)

There will be nothing more rewarding than a close intimate relationship with our Heavenly Father. When you seek Him with all your heart, you will find Him, it is promised. "You will seek Me and find Me when you seek Me with all your heart." (Jeremiah 29:13)

God's love, His grace and mercy are beyond measure, "And he passed in front of Moses, proclaiming, "The Lord the Lord, the compassionate and gracious God, slow to anger, abounding in love and faithfulness, maintaining love to thousands, and forgiving wickedness, rebellion and sin. Yet He does not leave the guilty unpunished; He punishes the children and their children for the sin of the parents to the third and fourth generation." (Exodus 34:6-7)

Not only is the Lord quick to forgive, He wants to bless you! When God blesses, people notice, and in your blessing, He is glorified, and people are witnessed to! "Yet the Lord longs to be gracious to you; therefore, He will rise up to show you compassion. For the Lord is a God of justice. Blessed are all who wait for Him!" (Isaiah 30:18)

Do not stop seeking a closer and more intimate relationship with God. He is infinite we will never truly experience all that He is on earth. The more of God you seek, the more your spirit will leap with joy as you find Him. The closer you become to Him, the more and more He will use you to be a blessing to others. I never feel more alive than when His life giving Spirit flows through me to be His hands, His feet, His voice and His heart.

"The desert and the parched land will be glad; the wilderness will rejoice and blossom. Like the crocus, it will burst into bloom; it will rejoice greatly and shout for joy. The glory of Lebanon will be given to it, the splendor of Carmel and Sharon; they will see the glory of the Lord, the splendor of our God. Strengthen the feeble hands, steady the knees that give way; say to those with fearful hearts, "Be strong, do not fear; your God will come, He will come with vengeance; with divine retribution

He will come to save you." Then will the eyes of the blind be opened and the ears of the deaf unstopped. Then will the lame leap like a deer, and the mute tongue shout for joy. Water will gush forth in the wilderness and streams in the desert. The burning sand will become a pool, the thirsty ground bubbling springs. In the haunts where jackals once lay, grass and reeds and papyrus will grow. And a highway will be there; it will be called the Way of Holiness; it will be for those who walk on that Way. The unclean will not journey on it; wicked fools will not go about on it. No lion will be there, nor any ravenous beast; they will not be found there. But only the redeemed will walk there, and those the Lord has rescued will return. They will enter Zion with singing; everlasting joy will crown their heads. Gladness and joy will overtake them, and sorrow and sighing will flee away." (Isaiah 35)

God bless you as you continually grow in Him, to the praise of His Holy Name.

Sandra Lott

Mama on Her Knees

Sometimes they need to see mama on her knees.

With all the love she has to give, she gives

the most when she's on her knees.

Sometimes they need to see the faith

behind her bended knees.

Mama goes to the Lord in prayer.

She loves her children so.

Sometimes they need to see mama on her knees.

She prays about their soul, she prays about their needs.

With all the love she has to give, mama goes to the Lord in prayer.

Sometimes they need to see mama on her knees.

Sometimes they need to see the faith

behind her bended knees.

Now they're grown with children of their own

and they're talking to the Lord on bended knees.

Other Books By Sandra Lott

A Princess in Waiting

An Eagle's Flight

Deep Waters Within

God's Love

I'm Saved! Where Do I Go From Here?

My Father's Eyes: Seeing Yourself through the Eyes of Love

Repairing Broken Walls: Restoring Joy & Peace-The Book

Repairing Broken Walls: Restoring Joy & Peace-The Study Guide

Ride the Wind

The Day Hope Was Born: God's Gift of Love

The Holy Spirit and the Baptism of the Holy Spirit

Children's Books

Tim & Gerald Ray Series: How Did He Get In There?

Tim & Gerald Ray Series: The Wind has a Voice

The Sheep that Went Astray

God Loves You!

Jeremiah. 31:3 "I have loved you with an everlasting love; I have drawn you with loving kindness."

I Timothy 2:3-4 "God our Savior, who wants all men to be saved and to come to the knowledge of the truth."

He will not knock on the door to your heart forever. Will you let Him in?

Revelation 3:20 "Here I am! I stand at the door and knock. If anyone hears My voice and opens the door, I will come in and eat with him, and he with Me."

Jesus is the only way to God.

John 14:6 "I am the way, the truth and the life. No one comes to the Father except through Me."

John 3:3 "I tell you the truth, no one can see the kingdom of God unless he is born again."

And, you must make Him Lord of your life.

Matthew 6:24 "No one can serve two masters."

Matthew 7:21 "Not everyone who says to Me, 'Lord, Lord', will enter the kingdom of heaven, but only he who does the will of My Father who is in heaven."

We must leave our old ways behind.

Mark 3:25 "If a house is divided against itself, that house cannot stand."

You can't live according to the flesh and desires of the sinful nature and expect to have Jesus in your heart. He is holy. He is love. Love and Hate cannot exist together.

Ephesians 4:22-24 "You were taught, with regard to your former way of life, to put off your old self, which is being corrupted by its deceitful desires; to be made new in the attitude of your minds; and to put on the new self, created to be like God in true righteousness and holiness."

God gives you the ability to do His will.
He knows it is hard.

Philippians 4:13 "I can do everything through Him who gives me strength."

Romans 3:23 "For all have sinned and fall short of the glory of God."

I John 1:9 "If we confess our sins, He is faithful and just and will forgive us our sins and purify us from all unrighteousness."

John 1:12 "Yet to all who received Him, to those who believed in His name, He gave the right to become children of God."

Romans 10:10 "For it is with your heart that you believe and are justified, and it is with your mouth that you confess and are saved."

Then after you confess and ask forgiveness and receive Jesus into your heart, you must testify (tell someone) and be baptized. In this, God is glorified, and others might be saved by your example.

II Timothy 1:8 "So do not be ashamed to testify about our Lord"

I Peter 3:21 "And this water symbolizes baptism that now saves you also-not the removal of dirt from the body but the pledge of a good conscience toward God. It saves you by the resurrection of Jesus Christ."

Invitation to Salvation Prayer

Dear Almighty Father in heaven, I know that I am a sinner and I ask your forgiveness of all my sins. I want to make You the Lord of my life and I want to serve You all the days of my life. I believe that Jesus Christ died on the cross for my sins. Thank you so much for loving me and waiting on me to come to the knowledge of the truth! Thank you for my salvation. Please help me and guide me in learning your Word so I can be a light to the world. Please, Jesus, come into my heart, and baptize me with Your Holy Spirit. I thank You, and praise Your Holy Name, and ask all this in the Name of Jesus Christ our Lord. Amen.

References within the Book

Author Sandra Lott

was born and raised in Texas and is the author of Ride the Wind, God's Love and My Father's Eyes: Seeing Yourself through the Eyes of Love and more. She has learned about the love and faithfulness of God through the death of her sixteen year old son and many other hardships. Through His love and comfort she has drawn close to the Father's love and has developed a passion for studying the Bible. That deep devotion to God in turn has given her the desire to help others grow in their understanding of the love of God and to grow spiritually.

Made in the USA
Columbia, SC
25 November 2018